THIS IS ABOUT YOU

Amazing, Weird, Beautiful You

Written by Mary England
Photography by Maura Housley

MASCOT® BOOKS

www.mascotbooks.com

This Is About You: Amazing, Weird, Beautiful You

This book is not intended as a substitute for the medical advice of physicians.The reader should regularly consult a physician in matters relating to his/her health and particularly with respect to any symptoms that may require diagnosis or medical attention.

For more information, please contact:
Mascot Books
560 Herndon Parkway #120
Herndon, VA 20170
info@mascotbooks.com

Library of Congress Control Number: 2015918615

CPSIA Code: PRTWP1215A
ISBN-13: 978-1-63177-448-5

Printed in Malaysia

*This book is dedicated to my coven, my dad,
the love of my life, and every woman who ever
doubted her own awesomeness.*

TABLE OF CONTENTS

INTRODUCTION

Hello Beautiful,

This book was made with you in mind! It's intended for you to use as a tool to fall in love with yourself and let that love grow stronger each and every day. It's a place where you will not only recognize how wonderful you already are, but also that loving yourself takes effort, especially at first.

In today's world we are obviously surrounded by a lot of pressure from external forces, telling us we aren't good enough as we are, pushing products down our throats to "fix" us. There's also a slow shift into a wider acceptance and general kindness in society. We're living in a time where issues of inequality are being addressed (albeit not quickly enough!) because we recognize that we're all worthy of the same rights and treatment! Why can't we take a lesson from this growth for ourselves? We, too, are awesome! We, too, deserve the best, and if we're not the first person to give it to ourselves, then who will it be?

As much new attention and momentum as this concept is getting, there's still not enough research on the subject. There are very few sources out there to explore, which is one of the main reasons I wanted to write this book for you. I also wanted to give my unique take on self love, which might be different from some of the other gurus you're familiar with.

I won't be sharing a step-by-step procedure to get you to a perfect life. The idea of a "perfect" life is elusive, but it's also drastically different for each of us. I intend on providing you with many examples of how to learn to love yourself, but more than that, I want to empower you to make your own decisions and stand behind them. I want you to fully understand that you're already beautiful, and if you're different than the rest, that's a thing to be celebrated, not hidden.

I'll never tell you to dress for your body type; I'll tell you where to find a crop top in your size. I'll never tell you there's only one way to do things; I'll give you options. I'll never judge you for your decisions; I'll only congratulate you on being yourself.

Also, I won't be sugar-coating anything. I believe in positive thinking,

I believe in self love, and I believe that we're all capable of a total transformation. However, I don't think these things happen overnight. I don't think you can wave a magic wand and your dream will appear on your doorstep. You have to meet the universe halfway. This book is about working on your part of that equation.

Life can be hard, but it's anything but terrible. There are way too many families who don't know where their next meal is coming from, too many women who aren't taken seriously or paid what they're worth at their jobs simply because of their gender, too many instances of police brutality that are based on racial profiling and too many people killed in war. I know these things are a part of our world and they cause me pain. I advocate for issues I believe in on a regular basis and I encourage you to do the same, but activism does not exist in a vacuum. You can protest with a positive attitude or while wearing a tutu. Being fabulous and knowing who you are doesn't mean you can't change the world. In fact, it makes you more likely to do so.

Not everyone identifies with my brand of silliness and color, or even with my level of optimism, and that's okay! I think there are still lessons in this book you can learn from and apply to your life with your own spin. Not everyone likes glitter, but that doesn't mean your life can't be sparkly.

I'll tell you my story first, so you know where I'm coming from. I tell you this as a reminder that you, too, can turn your life around. There is only today, and it's absolutely never ever too late.

1 MY STORY

LIVING WITH MENTAL ILLNESS

I was eight when I started blinking. Well, I guess I started blinking the day I was born, but I was eight when I started blinking; hard, violent blinks that lasted at least a whole second. I didn't know why I was doing it, but I knew I had to. I could put it off for a little bit, like if the teacher was calling on me, but then I had to pull my Lisa Frank folder in front of my face to get the blinks out.

Soon the feeling I got when I needed to blink spread to other parts of my face. I needed to turn my bottom lip out, tense my neck, nod my head forward quickly, bring my upper lip up to reach my nose, scrunch up my face as tightly as I could, roll both of my eyes to the bottom left corner, make this high pitched squeak in the back of my throat. It wasn't long before my friends started noticing, asking what was wrong and making fun of me. I told them, "I have allergies." I knew I was allergic to pollen from the previous spring. Maybe that was it? I had no idea.

Teachers called my parents. From my bedroom I heard my mom talking to her best friend downstairs when they thought I couldn't hear them. My mom responded to her friend's concerns about me with, "It's just a phase, she's fine." I hoped she was right.

I couldn't stop, though. It kept going for years. It earned me nicknames like "Blinky" and "Blink 182". One evening when I was twelve my dad picked me up from my piano teacher's house. I remember he was really frustrated with me. He told me to go home and look in the mirror and see how I looked. I got home and locked my door; I scooted my butt up to my floor length mirror and sat there. It was only a matter of seconds before I started making faces. It didn't take much longer for me to start sobbing. I looked terrible. How could anyone even talk to me? I was disgusting.

While all this was happening, I developed other quirks. I would have to turn the lamp on my nightstand on and off seventeen times before I could go to sleep, I had to lock and unlock my bedroom door six times every time I entered my room, and if the microwave said anything other than the current time, like if it had a few seconds remaining from an interrupted heating session, I would run to it as fast as I could to press cancel eight times in a row. Piles of paper had to be aligned perfectly; I walked with my head down so I could step on every crack and leaf I saw on the ground. If a drawer or door was slightly ajar I went insane. I couldn't make a full circle with my body, i.e. turn around, without "unwinding" myself. If I sat down and made a list of all the things I did it would be the half the length of this book. Each ritual had its own associated numbers . I envisioned members of my family and friends at school in extremely violent accidents. From an early age I unwillingly thought about very sexual things I didn't even understand. It was very unsettling.

When I was fourteen, I was reading the back pages of one of the magazines my mom subscribed to for me. I had quickly learned that the first eighty pages of each teeny bopper magazine were the same . They were all about make-up and stuff I didn't really know about yet or would ever learn to care about. There were always these interesting stories towards the end of every issue, though, and today's article was about a girl with OCD.

I read the words "Obsessive Compulsive Disorder" for the first time in an article that listed everything I did. It was almost like I had written the article myself. I looked around my room quickly, paranoid someone knew, but it was okay. I was alone in my room. But I realized, finally, that I wasn't alone in these thoughts.

Within a year, I had new friends, friends that would change everything. I spent every minute that I could with them, and we became very close. One day we were walking into a supermarket and one of them casually mentioned to me something about "my Tourette's". I asked him to repeat that word because I had never heard it before and then I asked him what it meant. He was surprised and didn't know what to say. He assumed I knew the thing that I so clearly had. "It's like, the name for all the blinking and stuff you do," he told me. I acted like I didn't care and quietly got my snacks with them. When I got home I looked up what "torets" was on my dial-up connection. After some Yahoo-based spell check, I realized that he was right. I had that, too.

To this day, I don't know if learning the names for my disorders made things worse or if it was just a coincidence, but the next six months were bad. Things went from bad to worse and the fact that I couldn't control my symptoms made me feel insane. I had terrible self-esteem and body issues. Besides the fact that I was in a dance company, surrounded by girls with tiny, lanky bodies, I found it really difficult to love the body that was the cause of so many other issues. I stopped eating for a while, losing a lot of my skin pigmentation and developing black circles under my eyes. Everything was spiraling out of control and I was depressed.

I scratched myself often. I would wear these rings with large gemstones so I could press them into my fingers. I pressed so hard I would break skin. I put holes in my ears in places I didn't even want piercings. Eventually I started actually cutting myself with scissors. As you might imagine, that didn't make things better. I got worse and worse. My parents started noticing I couldn't even make eye contact with them. One day I asked to go to therapy. I remember sitting on the kitchen counter, saying the words to my mom and her reacting strangely, in an angry way. I felt that I had to convince her that I needed help, but eventually I got it.

Within a couple of months I confessed to my therapist that I cut myself. She had a very unprofessional habit of eating lunch during literally every single one of our sessions, so I didn't think she would tell my parents. But I was wrong. I came home one night after being out with my friends and my parents cornered me at the door. They asked if I was hurting myself. They screamed. I cried. And they made an appointment for me to see a psychiatrist. At sixteen I was prescribed an anti-depressant which I am still on today.

Nothing really changed, though. I felt a little less sad, but not really. I still had all these symptoms that weren't being treated and an underlying sadness and lack of motivation. I hated my body and my brain. I wanted to die. I tried one time; I took half a bottle of aspirin and went to sleep. I had no idea that wasn't enough to kill me, but the point is that I believed that it would. I can't tell you how glad I am today that I was wrong. I woke up with only an upset stomach the next morning, but I wasn't glad.

I read young adult novels about people who committed suicide. I joined Livejournal communities for people who cut themselves. I wrote down my plan to kill myself on a yellow legal pad and began the note I would leave next to my body. I never finished the note and I threw it away in a public trashcan because I got terrified halfway through.

I remember standing at the top of the stairs one day as my parents screamed at me. "We can't go out because you might kill yourself while we're gone!" I didn't know what to say to that. I just screamed something back. They were at their wit's end, frustrated and not sure how to handle the situation. They got the phonebook out to call the local psych hospital. I cried and begged them not to send me there, and somehow I got out of it.

Towards the end of my senior year I started hanging out with a guy who had been my friend through back-to-back boyfriends. He was always there for me and now I was single he made his interest known. I didn't want to date him, but I sure loved hanging out with him. He made me happy. He made me laugh. I think that was the beginning of getting better.

There were plenty of relapses after that. I saw many different therapists and tried out countless prescriptions. I had an enormous number of panic attacks and dealt with the terrible side effects of the medications that were supposed to be making me feel better. Sometimes I would get really overwhelmed and give in. I knew people were watching so I got creative. I would hurt myself by burning myself with candle wax or rubbing something on my skin so hard that it gave me what looked like rug burns.

Eventually the relapses of self-mutilation and panic attacks were fewer and farther between. I found a cocktail of different medications that made me feel okay enough to function in everyday life. Things were still hard, though, and I finally decided to address one of the four diagnoses on my psychiatric face sheet with something called Cognitive Behavioral Therapy (CBT).

CBT is basically exposure therapy. If you're scared of a spider, first you look at a picture of a spider, then you sit in the same room as a spider, then you hold a spider. CBT uses the same kind of framework to treat anxiety disorders like my OCD. We would have talks about things that caused me anxiety, and why, and my therapist would give me homework assignments. I would go home and do the assignment every day that week. One of them was to sit in front of an open drawer and stare at it for forty-five minutes. Another was to put a table in the middle of my room and walk around it in the same direction thirty times.

You might be thinking, "If that was my homework in high school, I would have had a 4.0!" and I hear you, but I promise you it was the hardest thing I ever did. The thing about lots of disorders is that there is a part of your brain that says, "YOU HAVE TO DO THIS! DO THIS THING NOW!" and there is another part of your brain that says, "Are you insane? Why on earth would you need to do that? That's stupid!" The cognitive dissonance that dialogue creates is extremely distressing and I promise you that I know how silly walking around a table thirty times in a row sounds. I remember the first time I did it. I collapsed on the couch afterwards, my face, neck, and chest soaked with sweat and tears. I was in so much pain, but I fucking did it.

From ages nineteen to twenty-five (read: during all this mess), I worked at a psychiatric rehabilitation center. I got more experience there than in any other place in my life so far. I saw clients who had been sick for so long. Some didn't know how to physically make their mouth muscles turn into a smile. I saw clients who had no desire to get better, and some that simply didn't believe it was possible for them. I struggled many times with the feeling that I wasn't qualified to work there because I had my own issues.

Now I know that I was definitely qualified to work there. Having my own experience with mental illness made me more empathetic to the needs of the people I worked with and, more than that, having a mental illness doesn't automatically disqualify you from doing anything at all.

After six months of intensive CBT I "graduated", and that therapist now uses my story as an example of success for his clients. My current doctor, the one that prescribes my medications twice a year, once said to me, "Mary, I'm so impressed by your desire to get well. You have always wanted to get better and that's not always the case." I think that's a lesson in itself. If you don't want something, you won't get it.

At this point in my life, I still have four diagnoses on my face sheet -

Obsessive-Compulsive Disorder, Tourette's Syndrome, Panic Disorder, and Mood Disorder Not-Otherwise-Specified (think like, a unique form of Bipolar Disorder) and still take a couple of medications every day. I've successfully weaned myself off of more than half the meds I took at my worst. I'm extremely proud of that because it means that I've replaced the aid of the drug with coping skills that I've spent time and energy learning. It's not feasible for me, and many other people, to ever be totally off medication, and that's okay! Would I prefer not to have to remember to take a couple of pills every day? Would it be nice to know that my body can be its best self without the help of a capsule? Yes, of course! But it's fine, and I love myself not only in spite of taking medication, but also for knowing I'm important enough to seek out the help I need to be happy.

I'm very proud of how far I've come, but there are still days when I'm overwhelmed with anxiety, self-doubt, and depression. Sometimes those days feel like a giant step backwards, and sometimes those days make me feel like I have no authority to be writing this book. But the truth is the opposite is true. Mental illness is a life-long relationship for most people, and difficult days that don't seem to dazzle the way you want them to are a part of that relationship— actually, they're a part of life. Being able to remember the beauty in life while dealing with strong emotions or symptoms is a huge skill that I've acquired and I will help you to do the same. Sadness is not a weakness, and knowing both ends of the spectrum has given me a unique perspective that I hope to use to help you.

2

GRATITUDE & POSITIVITY

Loving life starts with loving yourself and I firmly believe that half of the foundation of loving yourself is all about demonstrating gratitude and focusing on having a positive attitude. Sometimes life sucks and it throws us more curve balls than we can dodge or hit back, but being able to figure out how to keep an optimistic outlook or not spiral out of control when too many problems barrel towards us at once is an incredible skill.

This chapter will focus on positive thinking, appreciation, using Happy and Self Love Journals, celebrating life, affirmations, and taking responsibility.

"Optimism is the faith that leads to achievement. Nothing can be done without hope and confidence." – Helen Keller

POSITIVE THINKING

Looking on the bright side of things is not something that comes easily for most people; it is absolutely a conscious decision and a devoted practice! I want to say up front, though, that optimism does NOT equal naivety.

Some people view optimism as a sign of stupidity, which is absolutely incorrect. As humans, we're naturally judgmental, and with judgment comes cynicism and doubt. We all have those natural reactions, but it takes a little practice and effort to find that Sparkly Lining.

My positive demeanor earns me a lot of criticism that my way of life is hokey and silly. That comes from people online who think I'm full of shit, as well as people I meet in real life who consider my beliefs are unsustainable. There are plenty of arguments from people who believe that thinking positively (and self love as a whole) is a bunch of unrealistic nonsense. You can probably guess that since I wrote an entire book on the topic, I disagree with that idea with the fury of a thousand suns, but I want to tell you why.

Self love and positive thinking is more than wearing something cheerful and twirling in a meadow. I mean, feel free to do that whenever you'd like, but bright lipstick and a fake mustache isn't fixing anything ingrained in your soul, nor is it doing much for societal issues like poverty, misogyny, or violence. Being positive does not mean blinding yourself to life's issues or refusing to recognize the negative in life. It simply means trying your very best to find the beauty.

If someone has the misconception that self love is that simple, I hope you can help prove them wrong. No one, including myself, is claiming that acting whimsically is going to cure depression. Self love is about caring enough about yourself, and knowing that you're important enough, to get the help you need to deal with your depression (but we'll get more into the mental health world later). I just want to make it clear that self love is all-encompassing and takes work. Finding the good in the world takes way more skill than complaining about everything you're unsatisfied with.

Positive psychology is a concept that is a bit easier to grasp than positive thinking. Positive thinking implies that it's necessary to think positively all the time, while positive psychology recognizes that there's a time and place for thinking negatively, or at least realistically. As well-adjusted humans, we need to be able to rationalize situations and make logical steps that ensure our survival and development. If there was an earthquake and you needed to find your family shelter it would be pretty stupid to sit there cross-legged saying, "The world sure is a miraculous place! Full of surprises around every corner!" That's wacky. Thinking negatively/realistically is something we need to be able to do! You can reflect on situations later and find unexpected blessings in things, but avoiding what's happening in real time can be straight up reckless.

That said, thinking negatively is a lot easier for us. It takes less effort and comes more naturally. I think we could all be experts on being pessimistic if we wanted. I don't want to waste your time, so I'm going to focus on positive thinking and how to practice it.

Scientific results have shown that optimism leads to overall better health, improved life expectancy, and success. There are enormous benefits to practicing a positive outlook, just as there are disadvantages to thinking pessimistically.

These things are cyclical, too. Putting good vibes into the universe means you're going to get good things back into your life. You know "Those Days", where things just seem to start out on a bad note? You slept past your alarm, spilled your coffee on your passenger's seat, and forgot a deadline for a project at work. You let these things affect your mood, and your mood affects your day. Maybe you're short with a coworker, your boss yells at you, or someone doesn't invite you out to lunch. Maybe you're so angry that you drive a little more recklessly and have an accident or get a ticket. There's a reason "Those Days" seem like nothing can go right and it's because you won't let it. You have the option, the choice, to start your day over at any point! Any time in the day, whether it's twenty minutes after your alarm went off, on your lunch break, or just a couple hours before your bedtime, you can decide to hit that figurative Reset Button in your mind and let your life and mood be a blank slate.

Now imagine one of "Those Days" where nothing can go right, except in reverse! When it rains it pours, and that goes for positive things, too. If you're in a good mood and smile at a stranger, they might strike up a conversation with you in line for your morning caffeinated beverage and give you their business card for an exciting opportunity. If you feel good, your mind is less cluttered and you'll be able to focus on your projects at work with ease and maybe even get ahead of stuff. You might be inclined to send a loving message to your significant other that will remind them how much they love you, which will prompt them to plan a romantic date for that evening. Good breeds good, so start the good within yourself, and wait for more good to rain down on you.

Positive thinking begins with seeking out the good in the world and within yourself. In order to think positively, you need to start training your brain to be able to see the glass half full, even if you don't agree that the situation is a good one.

STEPS FOR THINKING POSITIVELY

- **Figure out what you think negatively about over and over again.** When that topic enters your mind in any capacity, it will be easier for you to throw a red flag and know it's time to counteract these thoughts.

- **Be objective and give your negative thoughts a run for their money.** When you have an anxiety or negative feeling about yourself, counter it with logic. Does it make sense that you're ugly if just yesterday a stranger complimented you, or your best friend told you you're beautiful? Does life objectively suck when there are things to experience like sunrises, sex, and smoothies?

- **Stop surrounding yourself with negative people and situations that promote negativity.** Misery breeds more misery and not just in conversation! If being in crowds makes you "hate people", stay away from them! If listening to metal makes you focus on depressing situations, take it off your iPod.

- **Say nice things to other people (only when you mean them) every time you think of them.** Never swallow a compliment because it would be "weird" to say out loud. No one is ever getting enough praise, I promise you.

- **Remember that you can't control other people or the earth.** Focus on the present and release tension you're carrying and don't worry about things that haven't happened yet.

- **Take care of your mind, your body, and practice relaxation techniques on a regular basis.**

- **Give yourself room for mistakes, go easy on yourself, and allow yourself time to actually implement change!** Nothing happens overnight, and it's counterproductive to beat yourself up that you're "not there yet" when you're actually making a bit of progress!

- **Make your body appear positive.** Monkey see monkey do, fake it till you make it, all that jazz. Sit up straight, uncross your arms and make yourself smile. Making yourself smile for sixty seconds actually sends a signal to your brain that you're experiencing joy, so you trick yourself into a chemical feeling of happiness. It's not cheating; it's utilizing your resources.

- **Think about what you're good at in terms of self-control.** Do your friends envy your ability to only eat small portions, organize your planner every night, go for long runs a few times a week, or always put your laundry away while it's still warm? What are you good at doing? Approach getting rid of negative thinking with that same level of enthusiasm. Pretend that replacing a negative thought with a good one is that hill you need to climb, and high-five yourself at the top when you get there.

- **Schedule fun things.** It's hard to think optimistically when you're constantly working! Make sure you're adding cool things to your calendar as often as you can. Having a good time will put you in a good mood which will make it easier to notice good things. It's that simple.

"As we express our gratitude, we must never forget that the highest appreciation is not to utter words, but to live by them."
– John F. Kennedy

APPRECIATION

Recognizing and celebrating the things you already have in your life is a beautiful foundation for happiness. The best way I can suggest for you to begin expressing your gratitude is with a journal. Keeping what I refer to as a "Happy Journal" literally changed my life. It wasn't necessarily overnight, but it was quick.

I remember the first few nights of writing in multi-colored ink inside of that blank notebook I had hoarded on my shelf for years, and now finally had a purpose. It was exciting! I wrote down four happy things each evening and was satisfied with myself. Half a week in, I got in bed without writing an entry. I sighed to myself and begrudgingly got up to write in it. It started to feel like a chore, but I had a goal and I kept at it.

A little more than a month into the experience it became more second-nature to me. I would even start noting things that made me smile throughout the day. "I'll write that in my happy journal tonight," I'd think to myself. Then there was the first day since I'd been writing that I had a terrible day. My boyfriend and I got into a stupid, terrible fight and all I wanted to do was cry. What could even be good enough to write down in my journal today? It felt like everything sucked. I leaned up on my forearm and half-heartedly searched my brain for the good in that day. It actually wasn't that hard to find three things I was happy about, despite that dumb relationship issue. Once I wrote down just three short phrases I felt a bit better.

Making a time every day to take stock of the good things that happened in your day, or that you just recognized about life, will not only make you feel better about how you spent your last twenty-four hours, but it will make it easier and easier for you to find joy in simple pleasures in the future. The more you practice, the better you are at it, pretty much like everything else in life. It's not nearly as hard as solving a Rubik's Cube, but with minimal effort, it can reshape your cognition. So how do you start?

"Feeling gratitude and not expressing it is like wrapping a present and not giving it." – William Arthur Ward

KEEPING A HAPPY JOURNAL

First, you need to choose a system that works for you. It doesn't have to be in a separate journal or even on paper like mine. You could simply make a document on your laptop, or keep a note app on your phone. Whatever you choose, though, make it pretty! Whether that means purchasing a brightly colored spiral notebook or choosing a font and header that make you smile, make it a place that you enjoy coming back to each and every day.

Next, create a routine and stick to it strictly for a two-week period. Ideally, you'd want to stick to that routine strictly for the rest of forever, but we all know that life happens and the reality is you're going to miss days... just don't let that happen in the first two weeks! I find that's a fair amount of time to really build that structure. I recommend doing this before you go to bed, but make your routine work with your schedule! Maybe it's best to do it as soon as you wake up, or on your lunch break at work. Make it a priority for fourteen days. Then it will become easier to remember and eventually just a part of your lifestyle.

It's probably best to establish a minimum effort, especially in the beginning. How many things do you want to make sure you include on your list every day? Three, ten, just one? Make a goal and stick to it. I promise that eventually you'll list two dozen things without even lifting your pen for a break. Speaking of listing, it doesn't need to be a list! Just like everything else about your Happy Journal, make the format work for you. It can be a bulleted list, in paragraph form, or you could even draw stuff! Do you want to highlight key words, write every word in a different color pen? It's totally up to you! And your choices are perfect.

Use these prompts below to map out your Happy Journal plan. This can easily be altered as you figure out what works best for you.

What format will you use?

When will you write?

What will your minimum effort be?

Don't be afraid to include everything in your journal! Anything that makes you smile, laugh, or gives you goose bumps. It can be something you accomplished, or something that gave you relief. It can be something that was done for you, or something you experienced as a third party. It can be a thought you had, a goal you created, or a general appreciation for an aspect of life. As you go about your day, pay attention to good things and your physical body chemistry as you experience joyful things. It becomes conscious. It also helps to identify sparkly (silver) linings and become that "glass half full" kind of person. You can even start keeping a little note section on your phone for reminders of what to write down later!

(Examples: dancing with your friend, finishing your workout, not having to deal with a nasty coworker, your significant other buying you an ice cream cone, a stranger freestyle rapping in the street, the idea that all people are beautiful, deciding to stop smoking, or realizing how easy it is to get a candy bar at four in the morning.)

If you're feeling stale on Day One it might help to make a general list! To boost your confidence, start by listing everything you love. Keep going! Can you get to 100? To reach triple digits you're really going to have to reflect on your life, and tap into a part of your brain that you might not be used to using. This is a great preliminary mindset.

Use the spaces provided on the next 3 pages to try it out!

MAKE A LIST OF 100 THINGS YOU LOVE

1.
....

2.
....

3.
....

4.
....

5.
....

6.
....

7.
....

8.
....

9.
....

10.
....

11.
....

12.
....

13.
....

14.
....

15.
....

16.
....

17.
....

18.
....

19.
....

20.
....

21.
....

22.
....

23.
....

24.
....

25.
....

26.
....

27.
....

28.
....

29.
....

30.
....

31.
....

32.
....

33.

34.

35.

36.

37.

38.

39.

40.

41.

42.

43.

44.

45.

46

47.

48.

49.

50.

51.

52.

53.

54.

55.

56.

57.

58.

59.

60.

61.

62.

63.

64.

65.

66.

67.

....

68.

....

69.

....

70.

....

71.

....

72.

....

73.

....

74.

....

75.

....

76.

....

77.

....

78.

....

79.

....

80.

....

81.

....

82.

....

83.

....

84.

....

85.

....

86.

....

87.

....

88.

....

89.

....

90.

....

91.

....

92.

....

93.

....

94.

....

95.

....

96.

....

97.

....

98.

....

99.

....

100.

....

SELF LOVE JOURNAL

First and foremost, I recommend a Happy Journal. It's simple and pays for itself immediately, but that's not the only kind of journaling! Any kind of journaling is important and promotes appreciation. Art journaling sounds intimidating, especially for those who don't characterize themselves as artistically inclined, but I recommend it. Firstly, you are an artist and you are creative. We all are! Secondly, no one is asking you to draw a realistic portrait of the Mona Lisa in your notebook—we're just talking about doodles and pasting in magazine clippings!

A Self Love Journal (Bible, Book, whatever you want to call it) is a space you dedicate to celebrating yourself. Write down things you love about yourself, cut out positive power words from magazines that describe how you want to feel. Make a self portrait by gluing buttons on for eyes and using confetti for hair. It's actually really easy to do, but just like a Happy Journal, it's worth its weight in gold.

You can feel free to combine your Happy and Self Love Journals into one book if that's easier for you. For me, designating specific spaces for each task makes things more clear-cut for me, but you could make it a goal to add an entry about Self Love every night after you write down the good things that happened that day. You could incorporate those happy things into a drawing. You could just get one notebook with different sections so everything is in one place, but divided! It's all up to you.

Having a journal is not only good for being able to take a moment during the day to make your mind focus on the good, but also to have a tangible collection of the great parts of your life. You can hold that notebook in your hand, and know that its pages are full of the love that surrounds you and that you spotted it. You can also get this sense from any documentation you create, be it in an art journal, a scrapbook, or photos you take from fun moments!

SELF LOVE JOURNAL PROMPTS

- Your power word

- Advice do you need to follow

- What would you tell a large group of people?

- Quotes that make you feel alive

- Write an acrostic of your name

- Ways you can take care of yourself every day

- Things you can do to get out of a rut

- A positive affirmation

- Ideas for taking yourself out on a date

- Pictures of yourself and your body

- A self portrait

- A page that just says "I am beautiful"

- Start with "I deserve"

- Cut out pictures from magazines in your favorite color or of your favorite things

- What makes you unique?

- Write a (love) letter to yourself

- Paste in a picture of one of your idols and why they inspire you

- A list of things that inspire you

- Your dreams, your goals

- A list of things you're good at

"Life is what you celebrate. All of it. Even its end."
– Joanne Harris

CELEBRATING

Alongside of appreciation comes celebration. I look at appreciation as the cognitive aspect and celebration as the actionable step. Appreciation is recognizing something in your mind as being wonderful, for example a child dressed in elaborate black-tie attire, your favorite team winning the championship, the satisfying clickity-clack sound a typewriter makes as you press down on the old keys. Celebration is how you react to that recognition. You might walk up to that child and compliment her and her parents on the outfit, ask to take a picture, and post it to the internet with a caption about how much she made you smile. You might paint your face to go to the big game and scream for joy as you jump up and down in a side-hug with your best friend as your team scores the winning goal. You might just giggle out loud as you type a letter on a vintage typewriter and write more letters as a result of your joy.

Celebrating life doesn't need to be complicated. It can be as simple as adding one of those tiny umbrellas to your soda at dinner or hanging up a wreath on your front door to honor a holiday. The problem is, we end up thinking about celebrating as something that's only done for big occasions! Celebrating is bigger than Halloween and Christmas. It can occur way more often than graduations and weddings. Yes, those are fantastic reasons to party, but that doesn't mean you have to wait around for those events to pop up on your calendar! In fact, you shouldn't. Life is much better when you create your own reasons to party.

First of all, there is an unusual holiday for every day of the year. Did you know that May 14th is Chicken Dance Day and Wear Red Day is observed on the first Friday of February? There are tons of silly ways to celebrate these holidays, and by doing so, you're celebrating life. My favorite part about these holidays is that it gets you to focus on a detailed part of living that you might not have paid attention to in years. When's the last time you did the Chicken Dance? When's the last time you made a s'more? When's the last time you made your own musical instrument? I truly hope the answer to all of these questions is, "Uhh, yesterday!" but for most people it isn't. Making note of unusual holidays is a great way to get silly, pay attention to detail and make today special.

Making today special is the key ingredient to celebrating life. What's one thing you've done today that's a little different than all your other days? We usually have to do a ton of stuff over and over again every day. Shower, get to work, make dinner, pick up your kids, feed the cat, do chores, take your medicine. There's stuff we do every day to survive, to keep going, to not get swamped, but there's always a chance to do something a little different.

One unique act a day can keep your spirits up and prevent that feeling that you're falling into a rut. When we develop the feeling of being in a rigid, dull, unchanging routine we become discouraged, uninspired and sad. Realistically, we can't have a truly radical schedule every day. We can't drop off the map, become a nomad and dance with women in long flowing skirts with finger cymbals every day, but we can try to make sure that we do one little thing every day. Making that decision is celebratory in itself.

One of the most miserable ways to live life is on Auto-Pilot. We've all done it, pulling into a parking spot at work and not remembering the drive in. We pull ourselves out of bed after too little sleep, brush our teeth like a zombie, pour caffeine down our throats and do the things on our to do list with no intention. When we lack deliberate action we begin to accept things the way they are and forget about the concept of improvement. "Rinse, wash, repeat" is dull and when you think about it, there are a hundred ways to wash your hair without following the directions on the bottle.

"We can complain because rose bushes have thorns, or rejoice because thorn bushes have roses." – Abraham Lincoln

SPARKLY LININGS

A Sparkly Lining is the same thing as that term 'silver lining' you've heard before, just with a little more magic. When we're going about our day and everything seems to be going from bad to worse is when we really need to focus on finding a Sparkly Lining. All we're talking about is finding the good in a seemingly bad situation and doing so with a little more glitter, self-expression and general awesomeness. So how do you do it?

Bad things happen every day, and I'm not suggesting that when you find out someone was in a car crash or that your lab results came back positive you smile wide and jump for joy. The goal is to be able to hear and accept the reality of a negative situation and maintain control so you can find a solution as quickly as possible. Keeping a positive outlook can help you stay sane in the moment and react in the most beneficial way. After things have settled down, you might be able to look at what happened as a "blessing in disguise" or realize things could have been worse, which will help you not to fall into a depressed or hopeless state.

When my grandmother died, I couldn't function. I cried and walked around like a zombie for weeks. I held onto everything for a long time because we weren't able to have her funeral for three months after she passed. At her funeral I lost my mind again. It was terrible, and I had no idea how to make myself feel better about it.

Years later I've realized two things that make me feel better, one of which is more difficult to swallow than the other. First of all, I lived with my grandmother and she didn't want a cat. I was in the process of rescuing Bug from being put down by his previous owners and finding him a home with a coworker, but when Nannie died I was able to take Bug into my home and he has gotten me through more difficult times than I can count. Having this cat in my house has drastically improved the quality of my life.

Secondly, years before Nannie left us I had to interview her for a paper for my Ageism class. I asked her a question about life support and she looked around to make sure my dad wasn't in ear shot. She said, "If that ever happened to me, I would like to die." My mouth dropped open, and she told me that she had a life she loved and would never want to end it on a note that wasn't on her terms.

The day before she died she fell getting out of the car, breaking her leg in multiple places. She had to get surgery to fix it the following day and a blood clot moved to her brain while they were operating, killing her. A couple years passed before I was able to even think the thought that she wanted that to happen. She would have had to live in a rehabilitation center for months and, with her osteoporosis, her bones never would have healed enough for her to walk back up the stairs to her bedroom. She wanted to end life on a good note, on her terms.

I miss my grandma all the time. She was the kindest person I've ever met, with a passion for handwritten letters in purple ink and for life itself. I am in no way glad she's gone, but knowing that she ended life in a way better for her than the alternative, and that she inadvertently gifted me Bug, is what a Sparkly Lining is - finding the good in a bad situation.

I've heard people say that they've had to break up with friends who were too positive. They complained that they couldn't come to them with real problems because they would always find a way to spin it into a good thing. Yes, I'm serious. There are plenty of people in this world who would read that sentence and totally identify with it! If someone tells you they can't be your friend because you're too positive, simply smile and walk away, because guess what? It's actually a good thing. You don't need that in your life.

Feel free to empathize with your friends, but don't join in the misery. When you're responding to a text, e-mail, or face-to-face conversation, make sure you acknowledge any pain or stress your friend is experiencing, but then provide solutions! It's easy to say "that sucks", but ultimately you're just allowing that person to dwell.

I'm not saying this works for all situations. There's not really a good spin for someone experiencing abuse or the death of a loved one, but you need to use your judgment. We can all use time to wallow in the sadness and you can be a fantastic support system for your friends, but overall, further complaining or self-destructive behavior isn't helping anyone out in the long run.

We're generally better at seeing solutions to others' problems in a more objective light, so help your friends out! Come up with some ideas for how to make the situation better (and then remember that advice for yourself for later!). You also want to surround yourself with positivity and that includes people! If your friends are constantly complaining it's likely you'll fall into that routine as well. Find more upbeat people to spend time with. Take stock of what media you're consuming. Are you watching violent movies and news casts or listening to degrading music? It all has an impact on your mind and self-esteem.

I mentioned that positive thinking starts with seeing Sparkly Linings in everyday situations. That doesn't mean you have to agree that the situation in question is a good one. What I mean is, simply put positive thinking into practice. For example, every time you complain, groan, scream, or whine you should list at least two reasons why what's happening could be a good thing. Let your mind wander over to the greener pasture where great things happen! What is possible as a result of this thing that's stressing you out right now?

Is your roommate dipping out of your apartment early despite a verbal agreement and legal lease? Now you have this extra stressor on your chest, weighing down and causing anxiety. Scream, write down why it sucks so badly, and take a deep breath. Imagine you texted me what was wrong. Here's how I might respond: "Oh man, that sucks, babe. I'm so sorry you're having to deal with that right now on top of everything else! You have every right to be angry and anxious. This could end up being good, though! You could move out and get a place closer to your work and meet a roommate that is way cooler than the one you have now. Moving or getting a new roommate is always a stressful event, but it's also the beginning of an adventure that you wouldn't have had if your current roommate had stuck to her word."

Next time something bad happens, imagine you texted me. What would I say to you? I know your mind will be swimming with anxious thoughts about how you're going to solve your issue and that's okay! It's okay to let yourself be anxious and unfocused for a little bit, but don't let it consume you. By tomorrow you should be able to breathe deeply, state out loud why this could be a positive thing and create a plan of action. You don't have to believe in your heart that this is a good thing or that you're "lucky" to have it happen to you, but training your brain to look for the good is an invaluable skill.

"Never condemn yourself. Always affirm positive words into your life." – Lailah Gifty

AFFIRMATIONS

The next thing I recommend is to practice utilizing positive affirmations. Writing down a word or a phrase, then repeating it out loud can actually have a lot of power. You can use these words to reaffirm your own innate goodness, as well as the world's. Try coming up with a phrase or sentence that will make you focus on the positive, write it down and post it somewhere in your home that you'll see a lot (e.g. bathroom mirror, top of your laptop). Every time you see that piece of paper, say those words out loud. It takes less than ten seconds and it can reboot your brain! I like to write these statements down on paper hearts so it's also pretty to look at!

The first positive affirmation I ever wrote down was "I am colorful and strange in the best ways." Those are things that I tend to get criticized for, but they are things that I love about myself, so I celebrated them with an affirmation that I wrote down on a giant red heart cut out of poster board.

EXAMPLE POSITIVE AFFIRMATIONS

- I matter, and what I have to offer also matters.

- I trust the process in my life.

- I believe in myself and so do others.

- I deserve the best and most beautiful types of love.

- I am the perfect weight for me.

- I am beautiful and smart.

- Today will bring me nothing but joy.

- Today I will fully participate in life.

- Nothing will ruin my day without my permission.

- I am talented.

- My life is full of fantastic surprises.

- I let go of worries I have no control over.

- I accept responsibility for my own joy.

- I follow my dreams, my path, and my intuition no matter what.

- I only compare myself to my past self.

What is your positive affirmation? Write it down here, then write it on something else and post it up in your house, at work, in your car, wherever you want!

....

....

....

"Whether you think you can, or you think you can't – you're right." – Henry Ford

TAKING RESPONSIBILITY

If you're pessimistic about life, you're not likely to try new things. Forget about failure! It's all about the journey.

What are a few things you would do if you knew you could not fail at them?

1.
....

2.
....

3.
....

4.
....

5.
....

If things do go wrong, though, (wo)man up! Take responsibility for your behavior and the consequences of your actions. Placing blame on other people or external forces is quite simply a waste of time and energy you could be using to turn into your own positive role model. If you encounter someone with a life you envy, do something about it! Envy is often a call to action. You make your own decisions and choose your own path. If you know what a perfect life looks like for you, then begin taking steps now to make it happen. You have control!

I remember when I was about twenty, a girl I went to school with popped up in my Facebook feed. I clicked to her profile and saw this fabulous life she was leading. She was a year younger than me, yet she was traveling abroad in England and making costumes for plays. She was having themed parties and making friends with very interesting people. It seemed like she was utilizing her creative power every day and having the time of her life. I was super jealous.

Stalking her Facebook feed for a couple weeks, wishing I was with her, was not the correct response to that scenario. If there's something you realize you want in your life, that means you need to go out and get that thing, or at least try your damndest. Creating feelings of jealousy is insanely negative and will counteract your attempts at positive energy. When you see something you want, use that little initial fire of the Green Eyed Monster to inspire you to achieve a goal.

There are things in life we don't have control over. Actually, there's a lot we don't have control over. From the time you wake up till hitting your pillow you won't be able to change the fact that women are paid less than their male counterparts. You won't be able to end a war, rape culture or remove all traces of heroin from the streets. It's not realistic. There are not enough hours in the day and I doubt that a member of Congress or the president's cabinet is reading this right now, so you just might not possess that level of political power.

There are obviously things you can do to implement change in society, such as political and social activism, but real change takes time. Think about how long it took for women to be able to vote, for restrooms to be un-segregated and for people of the same gender to be able to get married in the United States. Unfortunately, radical movements can move at a snail's pace and until laws are made to fix so many of our issues, there's not a huge amount we can do.

So when I say that you need to accept responsibility for your happiness, I'm not telling you that you are in charge of everything! You aren't responsible for oppression against you for your gender, race or sexual orientation. You aren't the reason you were abused and are dealing with the symptoms of a mental disorder as a result. There are always things out of our control. There are always things that will try to shove you down and silence your beautiful voice. Your job is to do your best to rise above it, to make as much progress as you can of your own accord and to find the good in the world when everyone else is telling you how much it sucks. Be the diamond in the rough, the act that restores someone's faith in humanity and the beauty you want the world to be.

In the next chapter we will move from appreciation and celebration to methods of self care. Putting your needs first is imperative to a happy life.

THINGS TO TRY

- Make a list of all the miraculous things your body does on its own every day
- Set up your Happy Journal and write in it
- Create a positive affirmation, post it somewhere
- Any time you have a negative thought about yourself, immediately say two positive things about yourself
- Do the same thing for negative situations to practice finding Sparkly Linings
- Start a Self Love Journal and respond to your first prompt
- Remember that positivity does not equal naivety
- Embrace all emotions, but truly make an effort to laugh and smile often
- Eat dessert first
- Hang up twinkle lights and leave them up all year round
- Stop apologizing for your lifestyle or interests
- Roll down a hill
- Make a list of as many things you can think of that you love
- Compliment a stranger
- Sing while in the shower, driving and cooking
- Pet and talk to animals
- Be kind to everyone, including yourself
- Swim in a fountain
- Hang up your own art on the refrigerator
- Appreciate your ability to do things instead of complaining about small frustrations ("Ah! I'm flying on a steel bird thousands of feet in the sky!" versus "Ugh, I hate airplane food!")
- Never wait for an invitation to party
- Look up unusual holidays on Brownie Locks and write them into your calendar
- When you smell something delicious, stop what you're doing and inhale with your whole body

- Don't wait till people die to say how wonderful they are
- Bring your own fancy dishware/napkins/drink umbrellas to restaurants
- Turn envy into action
- Cheer out loud when you cross state and county lines
- Do one unique thing outside your routine every day
- Take the long way home
- Take care of the earth
- Never stifle your laughter
- Make childish jokes and puns
- Create a secret handshake with someone
- Say "How are you?" and "Have a nice day" to all cashiers, waiters, and toll booth operators
- Break out the novelty items you've been saving for a "special occasion"
- Draw a heart on your mirror so next time you shower you see it
- Bring fresh flowers into your home
- Do cheesy dance moves
- Stop judging others
- Learn about other cultures and appreciate what's amazing about your own
- Fight for equal rights for all
- Look at activities and chores as "I get to" versus "I have to"
- Give funny names when you're waiting for a table or a drink order
- Don't wait till the last day in October to wear a costume
- Marvel at today's technology and all it has to offer
- Visit nature/natural wonders
- Wear a lei
- Never say no to something because you're "too old"
- Wear your seatbelt, stay safe
- Reward yourself for a job well done
- Keep a book or digital document full of positive quotes

3
SELF CARE

Having a positive outlook and a healthy mind is a great foundation for practicing self love, and now we can move into the concept of self care. This is the next level, where you are making sure that your body is taken care of! Meeting those physiological needs is really important to staying happy and loving yourself.

This chapter will dive into the basics of self care and the effort involved, loving your body, using consumer products and spending time with yourself.

"Nourishing yourself in a way that helps you blossom in the direction you want to go is attainable, and you are worth the effort." – Deborah Day

THE BASICS

Your religion or culture might have placed a strong emphasis on the idea that you should behave selflessly, and that means putting others' needs before your own, turning the other cheek, giving yourself up, and letting someone else determine your path. It doesn't have to be like that, though. You can practice acts of kindness and selflessness while still taking care of yourself first! There's a reason those boring presentations on airplanes remind you to put on your gas mask before assisting others. There's no way you can help someone if you're passed out. Work on yourself, and once you're happy and healthy you can go out and help others and change the world! In fact, you're going to want to even more.

Taking care of yourself and practicing self love does not mean that you're lazy (nor is it an excuse to be). Deciding to say no to lunch with a friend because you need to tackle your own needs isn't selfish, and taking a nap when you're exhausted and can't be productive anymore isn't lazy. That doesn't mean you can use self care as an excuse to avoid life. You need to listen to your gut. If it's telling you to stay in bed, you might just need to stay in bed! My past experiences have indicated that I'm more likely to feel better if I get myself up and out of the house, but some days I really need to lounge and be grumpy. Your self care routine might not involve getting up and out of the house, and that's completely okay.

Taking care of yourself is a truly unique process. There are certain things that you should make sure you're paying attention to, but just like a nutrition or an exercise plan, it's completely different for every person. Some people need to make getting enough relaxation their number one priority and others need to know it's okay to take more time to recharge and spend time alone due to their introversion in a circle full of extroverted friends. There's no one thing I can tell you to do to practice self care. It might be a healthy breakfast drink or an orgasm as you're about to fall asleep. You have to figure out what you need the most and make time for it.

What are one to three things that are an absolute must for your happiness?

1.

....

2.

....

3.

....

"Caring for myself is not self-indulgence, it is self-preservation, and that is an act of political warfare." - Audre Lorde

IT'S NOT ALWAYS FUN

Self care isn't always fun. It's not just bubble baths and tall glasses of iced tea on a porch swing. Don't get me wrong, those things are awesome and super relaxing, but you also have to do work. You have to dive deep within yourself and find out what's bothering you at your core. One of my biggest acts of self care was going to CBT. It made me cry and question what was important. It made me angry and brought on more panic attacks in a six-month period than I can ever remember, but it was for me. It cost money, it took a ton of time out of my schedule, and I had to drive forty minutes one way in rush hour every week. It wasn't convenient, but I did it because I love myself. I wanted to feel better because I believed it was possible.

Self care and love isn't just a trip to the spa once every three months, either. It's not running your car into the ground and buying yourself a new one. It's taking care of the car you have like it's the only one you'll ever get. Self care is an everyday thing, an active process that takes energy, time, and commitment.

You can also use self love as a tool for protest. If you go online, it won't take you long to find a racist status on social media, and women can count on getting cat-called every day the same way I can count on my cat knocking over a freshly poured cup of soda. Practice self love for yourself, but for others as well. Say "fuck you" to misogyny, fat-shaming, ageism, and every type of oppression you can think of. Tell yourself you love yourself not only because you believe it, but because it might ruffle some feathers.

Tess Holiday is the first obese/plus-sized model to be signed by a modeling agency in the US. She loves herself without apology and she does it publicly. Every single day she gets hate messages, and people share articles and photos on the internet telling her that she should kill herself. Harnaam Kaur is a woman who has a full beard due to a side effect of Polycystic Ovary Syndrome (which I have, too!) and she has an Instagram account where she posts photos of herself almost exclusively. There are people who hate her and her photos. They're incredibly uncomfortable with the way she looks and even more so with the fact that she seems to be okay with it! They don't understand why she doesn't "just shave it off", and they don't need to. Women like this are challenging standards of beauty, prejudice, and acceptance in our society and it's a beautiful thing. There is no reason these women shouldn't love themselves wildly, and there is no reason you shouldn't either.

Loving yourself should be done for intrinsic reasons first and foremost. Loving yourself to piss someone off is like running before you can crawl. The idea of declaring that you're head over heels in love with yourself as you are is a radical idea, and doing so challenges negative things in our world. Kill two birds with one stone!

"You don't encourage people to take care of their body by telling them to hate it." – Laci Green

LOVING YOUR BODY

There was a really great experiment done where a group of children and adults were interviewed individually and asked the same question: "What would you change about your body?" The adults went first and gave answers that you'd probably expect. "I wish I was four inches taller." "I'd get rid of these love-handles!" "I'd make my boobs bigger and more symmetrical."

After the adults shared their answers, i.e. what was wrong with their bodies, it was the kids' turn. Their responses evoked a storm of emotion inside me, because they said things like, "I'd like to have a unicorn horn," or "I wish I could fly!" My hope for you is that you get to a point where if someone were to ask you, "What would you change about your body?" you would either answer that you'd like to make your skin polka dotted for camouflage or simply, "Nothing. I love my body".

Your body is kind of amazing, don't you think? It lets you see colors and dance around your room in your underwear. It lets you kiss the person you love and play Rock, Paper, Scissors to settle arguments like adults. Take a lesson from the kid-version of yourself and just love the body you're in! The love you have for yourself should be unconditional, babe. It doesn't falter when the scale increases in number or a pimple appears on one of your pores.

I'd like to clarify that if your answer to the above question is that you wish you were a man/woman, i.e. the opposite gender you were assigned at birth, that's a completely different story. I support gender identification regardless of sex organs, and I don't want you to think otherwise. Part of self love is accepting who you are, and if who you are is different than what you've been told to feel your whole life, that's okay. In fact, it's great! It's a tough road to start down, but only because of the stigma still associated with it. I promise you that there are more people every day who will support your decision, and I'm one of them.

It's also always okay to want to improve your health. Loving your body and yourself also means taking care of it. If your body mass index gets too high, you can start having health complications like heart disease, diabetes, and joint pain. Wanting to lose weight for health reasons, or even to fit better in clothes that you love is not a bad thing!

Loving your body and wanting to improve it are not mutually exclusive. Your body, just like your mind, is a constantly fluctuating and developing vessel. You can gain weight, lose weight, add muscle definition, get freckles, see cellulite disappear, grow hair, remove hair, sprout pimples, and keep scars. Your body is miraculous, and it can be what you want and need it to be.

Do what you need to do to make and keep yourself happy and healthy, but know that the road there doesn't need to be paved in criticism and self-doubt. You are already beautiful. Self-improvement is a beautiful thing, and I want everyone to be the happiest with themselves they possibly can be! But never put yourself down on your journey.

"Is 'fat' really the worst thing a human being can be? Is 'fat' worse than 'vindictive', 'jealous', 'shallow', 'vain', 'boring' or 'cruel'? Not to me." – J.K. Rowling

BEING OVERWEIGHT

As a child, I was always overweight. I knew I was overweight because I was teased for it pretty incessantly. When high school started, I joined the dance company and was surrounded by extremely thin girls. We spent four hours a day together, and if we weren't naked changing, we were just wearing leotards and tights. I became extremely conscious of my body, and just stopped eating. It wasn't really a conscious decision at first. I just thought if I ate a lot less I would get thin quickly. I was right, but when I realized I was right, I continued eating less and less. In the team photo of me that year, I weighed about fifteen pounds under what was healthy for my height. I also had no pigment in my skin and giant black circles underneath my eyes.

My body became a huge deal to me throughout high school. In addition to dancing twelve hours a week, I was also doing intense cardio and weights three times a week. Dancing might have been what made me more conscious of my body, but because it crept over into my (lack of) self-esteem, that wasn't the main focus anymore.

A couple of years after I graduated high school I started putting on weight. It coincided with the new medication I was taking to treat my symptoms of Obsessive-Compulsive Disorder and Tourette's Syndrome. The meds started working great, but the numbers on the scale kept going up and up. I had to decide what was more important, and I decided I'd rather have to buy new clothes and be bigger than be unhappy. I don't regret that decision in any way. However, as I gained more weight, I got worse about taking care of myself because I got more discouraged. What was the point?

I settled into eating fast food regularly and neglecting exercise, which only made me gain more weight. The few times that I got fed up and tried to diet and exercise, I couldn't lose more than ten pounds, so I stopped bothering. I became self-conscious about my new size and didn't even recognize myself in photos. I would avoid people I went to high school with when I'd see them at the local Wawa because I was worried I'd have to remind them who I was. I think the real issue was that I didn't remember who I was myself.

"You are imperfect, permanently and inevitably flawed. And you are beautiful." - Amy Bloom

ACCEPTING MY SIZE

I don't think I truly accepted my size until I went through a break up a couple years ago. I was forced back into the terrifying world of dating after seven years of being with the same person, and I didn't think I could cut it. I had done a lot for myself in the years leading up to the break up, such as developing hobbies that made me feel like I had purpose in life and quitting my day job, but my confidence was shaken. I had no idea if I would be good enough for someone to want from scratch.

I thought I was going to have to settle for someone I didn't find very attractive because they would be the only ones who would find me attractive. Quickly I realized that my size didn't actually matter with dating because I didn't let it. The kind of men I was interested in dating were awesome by nature, and that meant they wouldn't be turned off by my dress size. I could be with guys I thought were hot, and who reciprocated that feeling.

At this point in my life, I advocate for body positivity in a big way. My end goal is to lose a bit of weight, but only for health purposes. I want to live on this planet as long as I can because there's just way too much to do to have it cut short by an easily preventable illness. I was beautiful when I was tiny enough to wear children's T-shirts, and I am beautiful now that I'm twice that size.

I'm fat. I have no problem with that word because I don't use it in a negative way. I use it strictly as a descriptor, and sometimes I use it as a statement. I don't say "I'm fat" in a whiny voice, or to prompt a disingenuous compliment. I say it because it's accurate. You would never respond to your friend with, "Babe! You're not tall at all!" when she complained that a dress she was trying on was short on her body. Don't do that for your fat friends either!

We need to de-stigmatize the word "fat". The reason we naturally react to someone saying "I'm fat" with strong opposition is because we're told that being fat is bad. Plus size is far from ideal. Extra weight is disgusting. Once we accept that fat is just a body type, we can create a world where there is less pressure, more acceptance, and more options.

There's also no point making skinny people the villains. I despise ads that say things like "real women have curves". You know what makes you a real woman? Being a woman! You might have curves, or you might weigh less than a hundred pounds naturally. Your body is drastically different than your neighbor's body, and it doesn't need to be compared to theirs! Just because you're thin doesn't mean you're anorexic. Just because you're fat doesn't mean you're lazy.

In 2015, a few countries in Europe banned very thin models from participating in runway shows. Their intent was to help end body image issues and other things that lead to eating disorders like anorexia, but that's not the way to go about it. It's great that they want to shed light on mental illness and body positivity, but the way to do that is not to tell someone that their body is wrong! A fat person can be healthy the same way an ultra-thin one can. Some people are naturally tiny, and they have to deal with constant criticism and judgment, too! It's never okay to shame a body type. All we can do is promote health and acceptance.

You are beautiful now, just as you were ten years ago, just as you will be ten years from now.

"Low self-esteem is like driving through life with your hand-brake on." – Maxwell Maltz

PRODUCTS

If you're watching live TV, on a commercial break it's extremely likely you're going to see an advertisement for a beauty product specifically marketed towards women. There are thousands of products out there that make millions by telling us why we're not good enough, then creating something that will "fix" the problem they told us we had in the first place.

We're told it's bad to age, so here's cream that will delay or reduce your wrinkles. We're told it's bad to be bigger than a size four, so here's a band that will suck in your fat at night, or a pill that will speed up your metabolism so you can lose weight. In magazines, subway cars, and commercials we are told our body isn't good "as is". We need a lotion to remove our cellulite, hair dye to cover greys, and special underwear that hides our natural shape. These companies don't care if you're happy with yourself. They care about making money. If they need to tell you you're ugly to make money, they will.

It's impossible to completely forget the pre-established archetype of beauty that we're shown every day. Since you were born you've been shown (if not specifically told) that ideal beauty is smooth skin without blemishes, acne, or scars. It's a thin body with curves in the right places. It's shiny, styled hair. It's all these things we have to spend time and money on, because almost no one is this way naturally.

What I want to make sure we're doing as humans and individuals, is figuring out why we're consuming these products. Are you buying and using them because you genuinely want to or because you're trying to "correct" a part of you that you've been told is bad? Do you want to get rid of the dark hair above your lip because it bothers you or because you don't see women in Hollywood with noticeable mustaches? If you say that it bothers you, think about why. Your whole life has reinforced the idea that facial hair on women isn't beautiful, but why? Is that body hair making you uncomfortable or does it make you uncomfortable to think about how people would react to it?

If you were to spend the entire week in your house without seeing anyone, would you remove "excess" body hair? Who are you doing this for? Who are you putting on mascara for? Who are you wearing Spanx® for?

If your answer to these questions is a whole-hearted, "Me! I do it for me!" then good. I'm glad. Anything that makes you happy is worth doing. If you smile as you artistically apply shimmering shades of eye shadow to your upper lids, then do that every day! If you love running four miles every day because it gives you endorphins and it gives you time alone to think, then schedule it as often as you can! I would never tell you to stop something that brings you joy. My intent is only to make you evaluate why you're doing the things you're doing. Is it pressure from society? Is your idea of beauty aligned with the media's? It definitely doesn't need to be.

I've heard so many women say that they stopped shaving their legs because it's winter and no one is seeing them, or they're single right now, so what's the point? Think about that! Why are you shaving at all then? If you're fine with having hair on your legs when you're alone, then let it be! Never practice a beauty regime because you think you're supposed to or to please someone else. You are beautiful the way you were made, and it's okay to give the middle finger to the commercials that tell you to buy stuff to make you better.

The same thing goes for clothes. Everywhere we look we see things about "dressing for your shape" and making sure things are "flattering", and it's all ridiculous. Magazines still title articles as "Can You Pull Off A Crop Top?" and do outfit spreads for six different body types, the outfits changing depending on the model's proportions and measurements.

If your shoulders are broader, boobs are bigger, waist is smaller, or legs are longer than average, you can wear a crop top. You can also wear A-line dresses, maxi skirts, scoop neckline shirts, sweatpants, and string bikinis. If your face is round, oval, square, or heart-shaped you can wear any style of sunglasses and have any hair style and length you prefer. Media and the fashion industry have dictated what is "flattering" on us, and we're supposed to abide by that. You do not have to.

Again, if a specific length of skirt, cut of pants, or neckline makes you feel more sexy then by all means stock up on those clothes in your closet. Just never put something back on the rack after trying it on because it doesn't look "flattering". If you like something, wear it, it's that simple. I'm 5'8 and have a big tummy, love handles, back fat, D-cup boobs, and tiny legs. If I want to wear something that's tight in my midsection and cover up my legs, or necklines that don't highlight my cleavage (my two "best features"), I will. If I want to wear heels that make me tower over everyone including my boyfriend, I will. If I want to wear white after Labor Day or go in public without a bra, I will. These rules don't matter, and they don't need to apply to you. You have the power to decide what you put on your body.

Men need to practice self love, too. I single out women because at this point in life I think we need it a little more on average. There's definitely pressure on men to look a certain way, the same way there is for women, but it's just a bit different. For example, it's more difficult to be a fat woman in America. If a group of fat men wore Speedos and threw a car wash it would be considered hilarious or ironic. If a group of fat women did the same thing in bikinis it would be disgusting or brave. Men are held in higher regard in our culture, unfortunately, which makes it easier for them. They get paid more, are criticized less, and don't have as many aesthetic standards to adhere to. Men can be famous and overweight without a second glance, but it becomes an act of feminism for a woman. Heterosexual couples on television tend to require the woman to be much younger and traditionally hotter than her husband. Things like this make me focus more on preaching self love to women, but I want to emphasize that everyone should practice self love and self care. Gender should not dictate anything whatsoever.

So think about who you are when everyone goes home. What do you need to be happy, to feel beautiful? Indulge in those things and nothing extra unless you change your mind.

"I think it's very healthy to spend time alone. You need to know how to be alone and not be defined by another person."
– Olivia Wilde

SPEND TIME ALONE

Whether you're an extrovert or an introvert, you will still benefit from alone time. It should happen often, and it should be a conscious effort. By a conscious effort, I mean that it should be scheduled out. Sure, you're by yourself on your commute to work, in the bathroom, or even when you go to sleep at night, but that's just a part of your daily routine. I strongly recommend blocking out a couple hours once a week to take yourself out on a date!

When I started forming my interests and hobbies, like guerrilla art, I found it a lot easier to spend time by myself. In fact, most days I even preferred it. Don't get me wrong, I love my friends. They teach me things, go on strange adventures with me, and laugh with me. I enjoy spending time from them! I'm an extrovert by nature, which means I get my energy from social interactions, but I still really love and need Me Time.

How you do this? First, assess your current comfort level. Think about going out to eat at a restaurant or seeing a movie at the theater alone. How does that make you feel? If the thought of those things makes you cringe, you probably don't want to just jump right into that kind of extreme setting! But it's also possible that the idea of seeing a movie alone where you can spread out and not have to share your popcorn sounds intriguing. You might just have your first date idea!

Remember how I said to designate a time for it? Write it in your schedule the same as you would for a lunch date with a friend. Mark

SELF DATE IDEAS

- See a movie
- Eat dinner at a restaurant
- Walk around with a camera
- Visit a museum
- Go shopping for a new outfit
- Have a spa day
- Create a ritual
- Take a day trip somewhere
- Do yoga outdoors
- Have a drink at a bar
- Have an art picnic
- Take a class
- Be a tourist in your own city
- Just drive and see what happens.
- Go back to your hometown
- Check in at a hotel
- Write at a café
- Go shopping
- People watching
- Visit a botanical garden
- Go to a farmers market
- Take a bike ride
- Visit an animal shelter
- Have a selfie photoshoot
- Go to the library

yourself as unavailable! Write it down and follow through, don't stand yourself up! That would be rude.

Have a loose idea of what kind of activity you'll do that day, but really be open to spontaneity. One of the best things about being alone is that you don't to cater to someone else's needs. You don't have to worry about waiting for your friend to be hungry, or their allergies to nuts. No compromises need to be made for the time you're spending with yourself. Follow your instincts: go with the wind, act on impulses, engage with your environment. Check out nerdy stores your friends wouldn't be caught dead in and shake your butt down the street like Beyoncé! The only judge here is you, and I think you're going to give yourself tens across the board.

While you're spending time with yourself, and hopefully a few other times throughout the week, you should turn your phone off. Yeah, seriously. Have it with you in case of emergency, but turn it on airplane mode or shove it away in the depths of your purse. These days our phones are an extension of us, and it shouldn't really be that way. If you're spending time with yourself, you need to listen to your thoughts. It's going to be hard to really find out who you really are if you're constantly texting your friends or checking your Twitter feed. Free your mind from the digital connection you have to others. It would be rude to be glued to your phone on a first date, right? Don't be rude to yourself!

After you spend some time with yourself, take a minute to reflect on it. Write it down, talk about it with a friend, or just think about it. What was fun for you? What would you like to do more of? Was there something you wanted to do but didn't because of fear? Can you push yourself even further next time? Or was this your limit, and next time needs to be less scary? Cater to your needs and change it up to be the best experience it can be! Be open and vulnerable to this concept. Over time, it won't be as big of a deal (if it ever was).

Remember that you're always around you. You're the only person you have to live with for the rest of your life, and you need to make sure that you not only love yourself, but you enjoy being around yourself! You know that expression, "I love you, but I don't like you"? Make sure you love and like yourself. Would you be excited to meet you? I promise that spending time with yourself and discovering who you are and what you like will help the answer to that question be yes.

"Take care of your body. It's the only place you have to live."
– Jim Rohn

EXERCISE & NUTRITION

The basics that we all know and tend to either forget or push to the backburner are healthy nutrition and exercise. Those words have always evoked a taste of disgust in the back of my mouth, but I've learned that it doesn't need to be similar to trudging through hell; remember how to look at things from a positive angle!

So many things that are healthy for us are actually delicious. Load up on super sweet fruits and delicious steamed veggies. Treat yourself to one of those healthy green smoothies with a boost of protein or energy! Practice cooking healthy recipes, and tinker with them until you find the tastiest option.

I swear there are as many diets and meal plans as there are buildings in New York City, and you really don't need to follow any of them. Figure out one area you'd like to improve on in your nutrition and try to work on it. Is it eating small portions, more greens, or less sugar? It's so much easier to focus on one part of your diet than trying to uproot your entire eating system with a fad diet or brand new lifestyle.

Ultimately, eating healthier is a lifestyle. If you want it to stick you have to look at it as a long-term thing, but you don't need to measure things in teaspoons or keep a book to count calories. Just being aware of your food intake, cravings, and slip-ups is a great start. Honestly, just try to drink as much water as you can during the day and make sure you're eating fruits, vegetables, and protein. Eating a brownie or an extra helping of pasta salad isn't going to make you go up a dress size overnight (and it would actually be okay if it did).

Exercising can be even easier than eating healthy. I say that because I love food, but I love checking things off my to do list. It's harder for me to check off "eat healthy" from my list than "walk for twenty minutes". I can frame exercise as an activity in my mind, and by doing that I can also make myself feel better about some slightly questionable food choices that day.

It can start as simply as taking a walk around a park or your neighborhood. Begin leisurely and bring a camera, taking pictures of beautiful things that you notice along the way. Invest in a Wii and dance game that tracks your movement! You can get your blood pumping with easy, fun choreography to pop songs from the last five decades. You can try cheap classes for Yoga, Pilates, or Zumba, or just stretch in leggings in your bedroom. Play a sport in a community league, go roller skating, or jump on a trampoline! You can even dance down the street in your city wearing a tutu, putting on a show for everyone! Getting your body moving doesn't have to be boring.

Remember there is always a way to make something fun that you think will suck. Maybe this section isn't that one for you. Maybe you love working out and you can't believe I hate it. That's great! Add that to your set of skills, babe. Just remember that for any activity later in this book or in your life, you can always find a way to make the mundane exciting. You just have to look at it from all angles and use the creative section of your beautiful brain!

I know exercise and nutrition advice from a fat person seems stupid, and like the rest of the stuff I say in this book, you can always choose to ignore it. I will say that body acceptance doesn't need to be separate from healthy living. You can go to the gym three days a week and be a size 22. Health cannot be determined by looking at someone, no matter how over or underweight a person appears. I can't speak for everyone, but even though I'm fat, I still take care of myself. I am aware of things such as my sugar and cholesterol levels (which are, possibly to your surprise, healthier than some of my very thin friends!).

A pretty new thing is the HAES Movement (Health At Every Size), and it's fantastic. It supports and celebrates body diversity and recognizes that the war on obesity has resulted not in healthier, thinner people, but a lot of self hatred, eating disorders, and bad health. HAES offers a registry you can search to find professionals in all disciplines (doctors, psychiatrists, dance teachers, nutritionist, etc.) that promise not to criticize and shame you for your body, and instead give you the help and services you need. Again I say, wanting to improve your health or physical body is a beautiful decision! Accepting and loving yourself along the way is a vital part of that process. Love yourself, improve what you want, and praise yourself for that achievement!

What are five ways you can try to get exercise that won't feel monotonous or boring?

1.
....

2.
....

3.
....

4.
....

5.
....

"Too much of a good thing can be wonderful!" – Mae West

PLEASURE

Most of the time, when we talk about pleasure, we're talking about some sort of physical sensation. You can experience miniature miracles through your sense of touch, sight, taste, sound, and smell. Making time for pleasure is vital, and it's not only a great way to show you love yourself, but an instant mood booster!

Take decadent bubble baths in warm water mixed with Epsom salts and aromatherapy oils. Light scented candles and feed yourself a chocolate covered strawberry while you lounge in the tub. Check out museums filled with art that inspires you, or hit the streets to find colorful murals splattered across buildings. Listen to music that makes you want to roll the windows down as you drive, suddenly making you feel like the confines of your car are too small to express yourself. Let the wind hit your face and mess up your hair. Dance in the rain, order dessert first, and make super soft sheets a priority on your list of not-necessarily-essential things to buy. Treat yourself like a pampered princess, because you deserve it.

You know what else you should do? Take naps. Naps aren't lazy, they're productive. Forcing yourself to work through something by downing four cups of coffee to stay awake isn't going to yield the most innovative results. Rest is important for your body, and you need to give yourself that gift. Today's world glorifies being busy. If you want to get ahead, you definitely do need to hustle. I'm not denying that. If you're starting your own business or trying to juggle a full-time job, two kids, and a social life, something ends up taking a dip on the priority list. You don't need to be constantly in motion, running errands, and awake to be a valuable person, though. It's okay (and recommended!) to take breaks.

These may seem like fluffy, froofy suggestions and that's because they are. Pleasure is about being decadent and indulgent. You can't live that way 24-7, but making little pockets for it in your week is worth its weight in gold.

"I don't know the question, but sex is definitely the answer."
– Woody Allen

SEX

Sex and sexuality is a part of living, and it's okay (and important!) to acknowledge it. Everyone is different with sex. Some people can only have sex with someone who they are totally in love with, and that is beautiful. Some people love having random encounters with people, learning from different bodies and styles, and that is beautiful. Some people find all people attractive. Some people only want to have sex when it's with themselves. It's all beautiful.

What's important is that you're practicing the kind of sex that you want and makes you comfortable on a regular basis. Never let anyone tell you that what you desire is boring or too weird. If they don't want to participate in that with you they don't have to!

Masturbation is important. You can't depend on a partner for satisfaction, whether you're in a relationship or not. I was in a relationship for years where I thought masturbating insinuated a level of dishonesty with your partner. I can count the number of times I masturbated during that relationship on one hand. When that ended, a couple of my friends reminded me to make sure I was still having orgasms and exploring my sexuality even though I was alone, especially since I definitely wasn't ready to be with anyone else yet.

The number of toys out there for women is remarkable. There are things that stimulate any part of you that you might enjoy, and there's also a plethora of pornography you might like. I don't mean to say that everyone likes porn, because they don't. I actually really don't like it. When I started buying toys and learning how to pleasure myself I tried a bunch of different types of internet porn, even the ones that claim to appeal to women specifically, and it didn't do anything for me. I get way more turned on when I'm watching a TV show with character development and intimate moments. Watching Nick Miller kiss Jess Day for the first time on New Girl gets me every single time.

That's the whole thing, though. Sometimes you have to fail to figure out what you like. Maybe you love internet porn! Maybe you get off by reading erotic fiction or you're really into having your feet tickled. Figuring out what makes you excited is the first step, and the next is acting on it.

Most self help books I've read make sure to say something about how you need to treat your body with respect and reference the experiences the authors have had with any type of stripping or sex work as negative. They say they were "empty" at the time they tried erotic dancing or posing nude and they "know better" now. I don't think you need to be empty to try these things, and it's perfectly okay to decide you like doing them.

Obviously I think that any experience you have should be one you want to do for yourself. Pressuring or forcing someone into a sex act, performance, etc. is one hundred percent wrong and disgusting, but that doesn't mean that everyone who is stripping or performing burlesque hates what they do.

I've taken many burlesque classes and still really want to try performing at some point, but things like writing this book have taken precedent. The things I've learned in burlesque have been empowering and awesome, though. I've explored what I think sexy is in a full length mirror alone and in the presence of other women who were both teachers and students. I've learned traditional arts of seduction and decided whether I thought they were interesting or not (most of the time I don't).

One of my teachers gave us an activity during a class where we had to explore a persona that was out of character for us. Most of the people before me were assigned "silly" or "funny" to get them to try something wildly different than they were comfortable with. When it was my turn my teacher said, "Okay, I just want you to be classically sexy". At first I was offended. What? Why am I not sexy on my own? But I know what she meant now. My version of sexy is silly. The people who love me are turned on by the fact that I will abandon you mid-conversation to twirl in the middle of the street, talk about what it would be like if our bodily functions were glitter-based, and laugh while I'm kissing them. I'm sexy because I don't care about judgments. I'm sexy because I'm confident. I'm sexy because I'm Uncustomary. You are sexy, too! There are many people who agree that you're sexy. Your talents, mind, and body turn someone on and you have to remember that.

It's true that some strippers are just doing it because they know they can make a lot of money, and there's actually nothing wrong with that. I've always thought that if you can convince someone to give you money because they enjoy looking at your body, then by all means you should do so! If you're comfortable enough to share your naked body with a stranger, then you should be able to pay off your student loans. I don't care what anyone says. Get it, girl.

"Self-compassion is simply giving the same kindness to ourselves that we would give to others." – Christopher Germer

BEING NICE TO YOURSELF

Who is your best friend? Think about that person for a second. What do you love about them? What qualities do they possess as a person that makes them a good friend, and what physical attributes do they have that make them beautiful? Maybe they are hilarious, good at dancing, and have the softest hair you've ever touched. What about them annoys you? Maybe they're chronically late. Does the fact that they're always late make you not love them? Nope! You just said they were your best friend! You love them a whole lot! It blows when you have to wait for them to show up, but that doesn't take away from how funny, kind, and smart they are.

If your best friend came to you and told you she thought she was ugly, what would you say? If she just got dumped by her boyfriend what would you tell her? I bet you would be really nice to her. I bet you would tell her how gorgeous she is and how she deserves the best.

You've thought you were ugly before, though, right? You've looked in the mirror and pinched fat you wished wasn't there or swore at body hair you felt wasn't visually appealing. You've been dumped before right? Did you question your self-worth for a second? Maybe you thought you deserved to be dumped! We've all thought that stuff. It's kind of a part of the human condition, babe. But you know what you have to do? You have to talk to yourself the way you would talk to your best friend. Be kind, be consoling.

Having a positive body image isn't a linear line graph, where every day you love your body more and more without any setbacks. Having a day where you feel like you hate a part (or all) of your body doesn't mean that you have a bad body image overall. A meltdown in a fitting room over a specific size not zipping up or over seeing a photo of yourself tagged on Facebook in an upwards angle that makes it seem like you have six chins isn't the end of the world. It sucks in that moment, and you're allowed to feel bad for the moment. The hope, the goal, is that after you have your freak out, you realize that no matter what size the tag on your dress says or how other people perceive you, you are (still) beautiful. Give yourself a break for going ballistic for a second. You're human.

You are not defined by the shape of your stomach or your current relationship status, and you wouldn't believe that your best friend was for a second! She is an entire gorgeous entity with onion-like layers that surprise you and bring you joy every day, and SO ARE YOU. It's okay that you're not perfect. It's okay when you fuck up. Give yourself a hug and keep going.

Give yourself five compliments right now!

1.
....

2.
....

3.
....

4.
....

5.
....

In the next chapter we'll take what we know about self care and apply it to mental health. Keeping a healthy mind is a key ingredient for the foundation of self love.

THINGS TO TRY

- Put your needs first
- Try a dance game on the Wii
- Buy (or blend) yourself a green health smoothie
- Find a therapist and give it a try
- Get yourself a new sex toy and use it
- List the marvelous things that your body does on its own every day
- Stretch out your muscles, or try Yoga or Pilates
- Cuddle with a friend or lover
- Spend some time with an animal
- Get a massage, or give one to yourself
- Take yourself out on a date
- Make a delicious salad that leaves you full, not still hungry
- Take a dance class
- Get a pedicure
- Walk through a park
- Sunbathe
- Hula hoop
- Sit under a mood lamp
- Turn off your phone
- Reward yourself for doing a good job
- Take a B-12 Vitamin
- Make a sex bucket list
- Join a community sports league
- Try EFT/Tapping
- Jump on a trampoline
- Try laughter yoga
- Nap
- Lie in a hammock
- Make it a point to find five beautiful things on your way to work

- Have naked time
- Do a little (responsible) retail therapy
- Write a message in the dirt or sand
- Change your hairstyle, color, make-up, or clothing to reflect how you feel
- Cut back on caffeine and sugar, especially late in the day
- Let go of negative people in your life
- Listen to the playlist about self love at the back of this book
- Participate in a drum circle
- Limit your time looking at screens every day
- Take toys, bubbles, books, and beverages into the bathtub
- Actually take your lunch break (out of the building)
- Plan for practicing self care when you travel; don't let your routines fall to the wayside just because you're not falling asleep in your own bed that night
- Stop saying sorry when you didn't do anything wrong
- Make eye contact with yourself in the mirror and smile (it's okay if it's awkward at first)
- Accept compliments with grace, and believe they are true
- Write down compliments and nice things people say about you in a document or in a notebook
- Cross something off your to do list that you've kept on there forever but you're never actually going to do
- Wear fabrics you love touching so you're in a constant state of comfort throughout the day
- Plan out things the night before like your outfit and to do list so you don't have to worry about them in the morning
- Do something repetitive/tedious that you enjoy (cleaning, organizing files, making crafts in bulk) where you get a result that makes you happy but rest your mind during the process
- Take your bra off
- Buy yourself flowers
- Spend as much time in nature as you can

4 MENTAL HEALTH

Mental health is just as important as physical health, and reaching out for help for symptoms of any kind of depression, anxiety, or other mental illness is never something to feel bad for. There's an unfortunate stigma attached to mental illness, but I want you to love yourself enough to say who cares and put yourself first.

I'm not a doctor, I'm only speaking from experience. You are in charge of your life and always have the option to ignore advice. You don't ever have to listen to anyone. What works for one person might not work for anyone else. You know in your gut what's best for you, and you have to trust that feeling.

That said, if you are unhappy with the way things are and you have been doing the same thing over and over again with the same unpleasant, non-progressing results, it's time to try something different. That thing you try just might not be a suggestion from me. There's never any reason to feel like you're tolerating your own life. This life is something to enjoy, and while it might not feel like a party right now, know that it can be at some point. Always work to improve, because growing is a vital part of your human existence.

This chapter will examine depression, anxiety, general worry and sadness, toxic relationships and more.

"A lot of people don't realize that depression is an illness. I don't wish it on anyone, but if they would know how it feels, I swear they would think twice before they just shrug it."
– Jonathan Davis

DEPRESSION

In the chapter on Positivity, I talked about the power of positive thinking and why it's not bullshit. I stand by that sentiment with my whole heart, but this chapter is going to get a little more real about how depression can be one of the biggest obstacles in your journey of self love.

First of all, depression is real. We think that depression is a "lesser" mental illness than something like schizophrenia because it's more common. In a way, depression has become so de-stigmatized that it's stigmatized in a new way. We think we know so much about it because it's the most prevalent mental illness, but I've also heard some of the most ignorant claims about depression than any other disorder! People are becoming more opinionated about depression, not more informed.

Telling a person who is suffering from clinical depression to "cheer up" is about as useful as telling a person with cancer to "get better". Depression is as real as schizophrenia. It's as real as cancer. It affects our mood and personality, which ultimately affects our relationships with other people. It can be frustrating for someone to help someone else and not feel they're doing anything, especially if they don't see a "reason" for that person to be depressed. It can be more frustrating when you're the person who doesn't feel they have a "reason" for being depressed.

The thing is, you don't get a reason when you're depressed. It just happens. You develop all these symptoms such as losing interest, feeling tired all the time, and a decreased appetite but you can't attribute it to one specific thing. Some days you'll wake up and feel fine, and some days you'll wake up and wish you were still unconscious. There's no rhyme or reason, and even someone who has "recovered" from depression can still have relapses.

Sometimes there are specific events that trigger depression, like the death of a loved one, divorce, or homelessness. The depression you feel from these events is very real. It feels the same as someone who doesn't have a "reason". No matter what your circumstance is for battling depression, you're not alone and you're not crazy. Having a reason doesn't make depression easier; not having a reason doesn't make you insane. Being in an environment where your depression makes you feel like an outcast can make you feel crazy. Just know that you're not. You don't need to search for a reason to justify your feelings because there might not be one. You don't need to diagnose yourself and explain that you don't want to do something because of X, Y, and Z. Trying to find a reason might just give you additional anxiety! Today might just be a low day, and there's not much to do about it.

It's okay to have low days. It's okay to have low weeks. I know that saying "there's not much you can do about it" might seem counterintuitive to writing a self help book, but it's true. Too many books gloss over the issue of mental illness, referring to depression as being sad, telling you to go see a therapist, and move on. Mental illness is real, and it's shitty. It's shitty like having the flu. It's shitty like wearing your spouse dying suddenly. It's shitty like being diagnosed with Lime's Disease. It's not something you seek out, but it happens and you have to deal with it.

After figuring out that you're struggling with depression, dealing with your illness is the first big step. And it's just that: Dealing. Getting through it is sometimes all we can do. I was talking to my friend Janice about this topic and she said something brilliant. "Telling us to go for a walk or drink a cup of tea is insulting to our intellect. We are going for walks and drinking tea but it doesn't feel like anything." There it is. Yes, I will write out hundreds of ideas for you to do when you're bored, when you're sad, and when you're uninspired. Some days, though, you're going to look at those lists and roll your eyes. Some days you're not even going to have the energy to get the lists out.

It's okay to just exist for a while, to revel in your emotions, or to feel empty. It happens. Know that these feelings are temporary, and almost always you'll get a burst of energy, inspiration, and motivation to do something fun, happy, or new in a couple days. Honestly, as long as you don't want to hurt yourself or someone else, you can take this day to do what feels natural. Fighting what you truly want to do (stay in bed) can be counterproductive for your healing process. What's the worst thing that happens if you don't take a shower or run that errand right now? It's probably going to be just fine. As long as you can still take care of yourself and function as a (safe) person, it's okay. And know that eventually you're going to feel more than okay. You will shine.

If you stop taking care of yourself, though, it's time to get help. If you can't bring yourself to leave the house to get food or go a whole week without taking a shower, it might be time. Don't let things get out of control. Call a friend, call a hotline. If you don't have any friends nearby and you don't think a hotline would be helpful, get in your car or on a bus to go to the hospital. People in healthcare truly want to help you. That's why they got into that profession. Sometimes you might get a nurse that's having a bad day or seems more jaded than she should be, but you know what? You can ask for a new nurse. Ask for the head/charge nurse. Tell them how you want to be treated. They'll listen.

It's not time to give up. It's never time to give up. Remember that it's fine to take time for yourself and dwell, but before you think you've lost control completely, check in with yourself and try these basic things. If you can do them all for five days in a row, you're likely to start feeling a bit better!

MY SUGGESTIONS FOR
EVERY DAY GOALS

- Stay hydrated, drink at least four glasses of water each day (that's just half the ideal, you can do it).

- Eat at least two full meals a day, including protein and basic carbohydrates and feel free to treat yourself to something sweet!

- Get up and move your legs, stretch your body and take a walk around the block.

- Get dressed during the day and save your pajamas for bedtime.

- Turn on music. Laugh at something, this is as simple as streaming a stand-up comedy special on the internet.

- Shower. Have human interaction, hugs are important.

- Take any medications you're on.

- Give a compliment to someone else.

- Cross one thing off your to do list, even if it's just responding to an e-mail!

- Make bedtime a priority, where you turn off the TV, tuck your cell phone away, slow your brain down, and try to get eight hours.

I'm not a doctor, and I'm not telling you what to do. I will never tell you what to do. If you're not someone who benefits from forcing yourself to do fun activities when you're low, then don't. If you're someone who generally feels better by getting out of your comfort zone, then I will give you a ton of ideas on how to do so. I want you to know that being depressed might feel like a curse, but it's going to be okay. I want you to know that feeling depressed is acceptable, even though it's miserable. I want you to be safe. I want you to get help when you need it. I support you and your process. I respect you and your feelings.

"Anxiety is the dizziness of freedom." – Soren Kierkegaard

ANXIETY

Another prevalent mental health issue is anxiety. There are plenty of clinical varieties of anxiety like Obsessive-Compulsive Disorder, Panic Disorder, and Post Traumatic Stress Disorder. These illnesses are real, just like all the other ones I've listed and can be just as crippling. (Actually from here on out, just assume that all illnesses are real!) The level of severity of anxiety disorders ranges the same way it does with depression and anything else on this earth, but it can get so bad that you don't want to leave the house out of fear.

Dealing with anxiety is a bit different than depression. Although it ebbs and flows the same was depression does, the underlying worry and fear tends to linger no matter what. Some days you might wake up a little more confident and tackle stuff you wouldn't have been able to even think about last Wednesday, but that anxiety is still in the back of your mind.

Having gone through Cognitive-Behavioral Therapy, I can say that exposure to anxiety is a very helpful tool. I absolutely recommend you get the aid of a professional because it's hard and it sucks. You need someone who can help you through it. You end up putting yourself in feelings that cause you anxiety and you learn to "sit" with that feeling. The more frequently you "sit with your anxiety", the less terrifying it becomes.

I had to do so many exercises to nip my rituals in the bud. Years later, I can do a 360 spin without unwinding myself or a see a microwave timer on anything but zero and not run over to press the cancel button eight times in a row, but it still hurts me a little. I still want to do those things, but the difference is I don't anymore.

That's what I meant earlier about mental illness being a life-long relationship. Maybe I don't exhibit the physical symptoms of OCD anymore, but I still want to do them. I still have those thoughts. I'm just able to control them now. It's not ideal. I would obviously like to rid myself of the thoughts completely, but that's not going to happen. Accepting that's part of my life actually causes less anxiety for me because I'm not using my brain power to worry about the fact that I have anxiety. You can have anxiety about your anxiety, so accepting it as a part of you really frees up some space in your mind.

The advice I gave for depression goes double for anxiety. If your social anxiety is telling you that going to a concert or party would make you miserable, it's okay to disappoint your friends and tell them you're staying in tonight. Your needs come first. However, if you get to the point where you're calling out of work or not able to take basic care of yourself, it's time to reach out to a resource that can help you. There are many in place, and if you have access to the internet and/or a phone, you can find almost all of them.

"I've had a lot of worries in my life, most of which never happened" – Mark Twain

WORKING ON WORRYING & COMBATING SADNESS

Maybe you don't have a clinical form of depression or anxiety, but we all deal with bouts of sadness and worry. I know lots of people who over-analyze everything, and spend hours every day thinking and worrying about things they can't control. Tossing and turning at night, worrying about a project at work the next day causes you to lose sleep which makes everything harder once you do wake up. Going over everything a million different ways in your head while you're driving to a first date, and creating fictional scenarios of how things will go wrong will only make you nervous and not act like yourself when you finally meet them. What's the solution? Don't worry. Easier said than done, right? Learning not to worry is similar to the framework I laid out for overcoming serious anxiety. It takes a lot of practice.

Figure out what you worry about. Is it relationships, work, weather, everything? Do you have any control over them?

Once you have the answers to those questions, break the worries into two categories: things you have control over and things you don't. It's likely that there will be more in the latter category, and that's what we're going to focus on. If you're spending a lot of time worrying about things that you can change, we'll tackle that more in the last chapter about making goals and implementing change in your life.

There are two main things we can't control: the physical earth and other people. There is nothing you can do to prevent an earthquake, or an asshole texting on his cell phone from barreling through a red light and crashing into your car. All we can do is prepare, but don't go nuts with preparations! For example, it's definitely a good idea to have canned foods, flash lights, and bottled water in your house in case of an emergency, but you shouldn't dedicate hours every week to making sure that you have some sort of apocalypse plan in case of a zombie attack. Wear your seatbelt, stay alert while driving, and do your best to anticipate other drivers. If you're worried about someone who is swerving in between lanes, get away from them. If someone is hell bent on crashing into your car, they'll probably find a way without your consent.

You can't waste your life worrying about things that haven't happened yet. Prepare, yes. Dread, no. If a disaster occurs, you'll adapt! Make sure you have resources in place, like keeping your cell phone charged, a full gas tank, and having a spare tire in your trunk, but then let it go. Prepare, then release. For example, having an allergy to peanuts is something you have to incorporate into your daily life. Don't eat at places that use peanut oil, read warning labels, and carry an epi pen, but don't spend all day daydreaming about what would happen if you had a reaction. It doesn't help anything, including your stress level.

Figuring out why you're worrying is a big task. What's at the root of this worry? Do you feel like you need to be in control of everything? Are you a perfectionist? Do you have low self-esteem that makes you assume you'll be treated poorly? Figuring out the reason for your anxiety is an important key to decreasing it.

My Suggestion: Next time you have a worry and are about to spin into a fit of anxiety of over-thinking, do something immediately to distract yourself and focus on that activity. Chances are, while you're working on that activity, your brain is still going to try to think about the thing you're trying not to think about. It's okay. Accept those thoughts, but keep trying to do the new activity. Maybe it's singing loudly along with a song, untying a knot, doing the Macarena, saying the alphabet backwards, stretching your muscles, or naming the Seven Dwarves. Use all your energy to keep doing that new thing. You'll feel anxious not allowing yourself to think about it, but the more times you try to distract yourself the easier it will be. Eventually you might not even need to distract yourself anymore.

In the same vein of non-clinical anxiety, you can experience waves of the blues without being diagnosed with depression. In less severe cases, my go-to is to get up and do something. When I'm circumstantially sad, all I want to do is lie in my bed in pajamas, eat pasta and desserts while binge-watching TV shows I've already seen forty times. I forget that as soon as I leave the house, miraculous things happen. I've had very few episodes of serendipity sitting in my bedroom. There's an entire world out there full of strangers to observe, foods to eat, and roads to explore. Taking myself out just for two hours almost always enhances my mood. It might not fix me, but I'll feel a lot better about my day, and something fun might happen while I'm out! You never know, so you might as well try.

Remember though, it is acceptable to have a Sad Day! Look inward, and decide if this is a funk you could easily snap yourself out of or if dwelling in the sweet misery makes you feel better right now. Honestly, sometimes I get sick of being sad. Sometimes I will allow myself to be sad just because I know it will get boring eventually. Let's face it: lying in bed aimless, going over the same thing in your head an infinite number of times is pretty dreadful. By the time I have to get up to use the bathroom again, I might decide I have to get out of the house or I'll go crazy, and that's when the rise out of my funk begins.

"Don't stand in your own way." - Unknown

SELF SABOTAGE

The journey of self love has a lot of "rest stops" where we're presented with the opportunity to sabotage ourselves. I'm not going to lie to you, sabotaging yourself can be really fun in the moment. I've lay on my couch in the fetal position, fantasizing about hurting myself, wondering what it would be like to have a total breakdown were I to go back on a ton of medication that zonks me out every day. It sounds awesome in that second. When you've been depressed for large chunks of time, it becomes a place of familiarity, an alluring escape. I don't want to be depressed, but knowing that I could be is comforting for some reason. You and I aren't the only ones who think about that.

Sabotaging yourself doesn't need to be drastic, though. It's not always mutilation or taking an excessive number of pills. When I talk about sabotage, I'm referring to anything that you do when your body knows, on some level, it's not the best idea for you. For example, maybe that's getting really drunk without a plan for how to get home or trying a new drug in an environment that doesn't feel safe to you. It might be having sex with a stranger without protection, or charging a bunch of clothes to your credit card when you don't have the money to pay for it. It could just be staying out later than you wanted to, depriving yourself of a much needed night's sleep, or saying yes to a favor for a friend that's definitely going to cause you a lot of anxiety.

We all have different vices, from smoking cigarettes to eating family-sized portions of macaroni and cheese at two in the morning. We all know that feeling of a twinge of guilt as we give in to doing that thing that feels really amazing in the moment, but we might regret it in the morning or five years from now.

In psychology, we use the term 'id' to describe the part of our psyche that wants what it wants now! Imagine a toddler who wants that candy bar, or a baby who is screaming because she's tired. It's that basic, simple part of our mind that wants instant gratification. It's so easy to give in to our id! It's much easier to say yes to an impulse than to suppress it.

The term 'ego' is what we'd use to describe how we satisfy the id in a realistic way that's going to help you out long-term. That's much harder, but much better for you. Are you having an intense craving for sugar? Maybe you could eat some strawberries instead to satisfy that urge, or just break off a square from your chocolate bar instead of eating five hundred calories worth of it. Making decisions that will make you happier in the long-run is a huge act of self love.

Have you ever had the thought, "If I had run just half a mile every day for the past two years, I'd have lost so much weight by now"? It's kind of like that. There's nothing I can do about the past two years, but what I can do is start running half a mile every day starting right now. Making a choice to do something that's going to make you much happier next week or next year is an incredibly mature thing, and one that will bring you much happiness and pride.

Yeah, it sucks to not give into your urges. If you cave, don't beat yourself up! What really sucks is giving in to an urge and feeling so guilty about it that you fall down the rabbit hole, committing even more acts of self-sabotage to temporarily alleviate the negative feelings you have. That's a slippery slope. I've fallen off the healthy eating wagon with some complex carbohydrates and felt so bad about it that I gave in hard core and just made a giant plate of food that would rival the daily caloric intake of the most decorated Olympic athlete of all time.

Remember that it's much better to just do that one impulsive thing and get it out of your system, forgive yourself, and move on. The easier you are on yourself, the easier it will be to make the better decision next time. Part of self love is figuring out how to be nice to yourself and forgive your actions.

There's always a part of ourselves that knows what's good for us, and a part that wants to do the opposite anyway. That's okay, that's normal, and honestly being bad for a hot second is fun and kind of healthy in my opinion. If all you ever did was eat salads with low fat dressing, wash your make-up off before going to bed early, and never break the rules, life would be a little duller. It's okay to get crazy every once in a while, It adds character and gives you a story that makes you feel like an interesting, well-rounded human! Just always be safe, and know that you can't go ape-shit every day. Those moments of recklessness should be few and far between, but know you're not wrong for craving them.

What are three ways you tend to self-sabotage?

1.

....

2.

....

3.

....

What are two things you can do instead of doing those things next time?

1A.

....

1B.

....

2A.

....

2B.

....

3A.

....

3B.

....

"You are allowed to terminate toxic relationships. You are allowed to walk away from people who hurt you. You are allowed to be angry and selfish and unforgiving. You don't owe anyone an explanation for taking care of yourself." - Unknown

TOXIC RELATIONSHIPS

I went for years without speaking to my mother even though she lived less than five miles away from me. I moved myself out of an environment I found to be unhealthy, and took several years to heal, grow, and move on. I talk to my mom now, and a lot of it is because she's changed a lot; she did some growing, too. It's easier for me to interact with her now that I have a higher self-esteem and know that I don't need to stick out any situations that I don't want to just because I feel like I should.

I don't think it would have been possible for me to build my self-esteem if I was living with her during those years. I needed to step away. I'm glad I did, and I'm glad I gave it a second chance years later when I felt able to, but I want to let you know that just because someone is family doesn't mean you owe them anything.

That's a tough thing to swallow, I know, especially when it's a parent, someone who raised you, clothed you, provided you a home. If they really love you, support you, and want you to be happy, then they will be able to respect your decision for distance if you choose that to be something you need. The same thing goes for siblings, cousins, aunts, grandparents, everyone. If someone is providing you with a toxic environment that is preventing you from reaching your potential, you don't need to stay with them, be it residence or contact-wise.

Your family is whom you choose to love and surround yourself with. Lots of times that includes a significant other, and a romantic partner is a unique thing. They become someone you share more with than anyone else, developing trust and an intimate connection. Sometimes, though, those relationships become toxic, too. Obviously if your significant other is being unfaithful in a monogamous situation, lying to you, or abusing you in any way, that's a toxic environment you need to escape.

It doesn't need to be that severe, though. Being in a relationship with someone who hinders your innate beauty is terrible, too. Does your partner tell you your interests are stupid? Do they make you feel small? Do they pick fights with you? Or maybe you're the one doing one of these things. Fighting all the time is not good, and it usually means it's time to move on. We all know fighting is healthy and good in small doses, it demonstrates passion! That said, you should be more happy than miserable in all relationships, especially romantic. The good times should always far outweigh the bad. That doesn't mean if you're having a problem you should throw your hands in the air and give up. But if you find yourself in the same arguments over and over, you need to love yourself enough to leave.

Loving yourself enough to exit a relationship is a huge deal. It's hard, always. Sometimes it's as simple as removing a number from your phone, but sometimes you have to get a new bank account and find a different place to live. It's never fun or easy to move on, but practicing self love means respecting your time and mental health enough to not put yourself in situations that cause you emotional turmoil.

Recently I've realized the importance of only surrounding myself with people who inspire me or make me happy in some way. Even if you've been friends with someone for a decade, it's okay to distance yourself from them if they're excessively negative, always complaining, or cause you anxiety by their inconsiderate or irresponsible nature. I've started taking responsibility for bad experiences with people whom I know I shouldn't be hanging out with. If I always complain about someone after I see them, but then I agree to hang out with them again, what happens is on me! I'm the one putting myself back in that situation, and I know better. It sucks to have to say no to people who care about you. Not wanting to be around someone doesn't mean you don't care about them, it just means that you're choosing positivity in your life.

Once I dated a guy for two months and he fell off the face of the earth without explanation. Six weeks later, he came back and explained that his ex contacted him and he wanted to try to make it work with her. I forgave him and we dated for a few more months before he disappeared again. Six weeks after that, he called me to tell me he had actually been cheating on his girlfriend of five years with me. I realized everything he told me was a lie, from where he was during the day to every "I love you". I contacted his girlfriend to let her know what happened and that was the end of it.

About a year later, he messaged me because he felt like he owed me a thank you. He said he had found someone new, whom he truly loved, and he never would have found her without me. He said he was sorry for how he treated me, wanted to see me and explain things to make amends. He called, texted, requested to be my friend on Facebook, and liked my public photos in a twenty-minute period. I told him I wasn't interested in talking to him, and he got angry. All of a sudden I felt this weird guilt. The altruistic side of me wanted to forgive him and let him explain, to allow him back in my life because maybe he truly had changed. I felt like I was being mean for denying him.

When we were dating, I knew what was going on. Maybe not completely consciously, but I asked him multiple times if there was something going on or if he was still seeing his ex. There were an enormous number of red flags, and I ignored all of them because I was in a place where I just wanted to be loved so desperately. It hurts me to know I did that to myself, that I accepted a lesser love than I really deserved because of my lack of self-worth at the time, and I know that having him in my life would only remind me of that.

The reality is, I gave him way too many chances and there was no reason for him to reach out. In his mind, he might think he was doing the "right thing", but that doesn't mean I'm required to let him into my life on anything but my own terms. I'm a nice person, so it was hard for me to be mean to someone regardless of the circumstances, but it was more important that I kept him out of my life than get walked all over.

Forgiveness is a beautiful thing. We need it in our lives, but it's not a black and white situation. You never need to let someone (back) into your life on someone else's terms or without your permission. You are the star of the show here, the leading lady, and you get to decide the casting list in your life.

"Eating disorders are like a gun that's formed by genetics, loaded by a culture and family ideals, and triggered by unbearable distress." – Aimee Liu

EATING DISORDERS

Today, we have an excessive amount of pressure from the media, society, and even our friends to look a certain way. The ideal body type, especially for women, changes every few years and creates an unrealistic and unattainable framework for physical beauty. The main problem isn't just that we're told how big our boobs, butt, and waist should be, but that physical beauty is prioritized well above who we are as people.

No, there shouldn't be an "ideal body type" that makes people feel inadequate. There should be way more push to celebrate who we are as individuals. If we were to place more emphasis on our unique talents, intelligence, skills, traits, and quirks, we wouldn't have as much time to fret that our body isn't good enough.

By now, you know that the models we see on magazines are a joke. You know they are photoshopped almost 100% of the time. You know that in order to have a body that fits into a size zero (when that's not your natural shape), you need to adopt a miserable lifestyle of barely feeding yourself and exercising excessively. You know all this stuff, but you can still feel inadequate when you compare your naked body in the mirror to what you see on the internet.

These pressures have pushed way too many women into unhealthy eating patterns that lead to eating disorders like anorexia nervosa and bulimia nervosa. Girls will do anything to lose weight. They can get so skinny and sick that their organs start failing. They can look their 90-pound-self in the mirror and still see a fat unworthy person.

Body dysmorphia, which is basically when you see a distorted version of your body, plays a lot into eating disorders. An obvious example is someone who is clearly skin and bones but still believes she is fat, but it's not always that severe. Some people become fixated on one part of their body to the point they will perform surgery on themselves to replace the cartilage in their nose so it takes on a different shape. Sometimes it's as simple as thinking people are going to judge you when you go outside. You might think your arms are hideous, and interacting with someone in anything but a baggy sweatshirt is going to repulse your friends and strangers. You might leave events early because you are uncomfortable and imagine that people can't stop staring at your not-so-buttery complexion.

Eating disorders and body dysmporphia severely alter the way sufferers of the affliction live their lives. I've found that most women I've known battle with their appearance, on some level, be it diagnosable or not. They enter a fit of anxiety about what outfit to wear to hide a blemish or appear slimmer. They spend hoards of money on products to alter their appearance. Why are we doing this? Who is it for?

If you are dealing with these types of issues, my advice to you is definitely to start inside. Work on your self-esteem first. Figure out what you're good at and why you have wonderful value. Once you have a bit more confidence, push your boundaries a little. I've found that spending time naked improves my confidence immensely, even when I'm alone! Just doing things naked at home by myself makes me realize that it's really not so bad. My body is my body and it can do all the things I need it to do, whether it's covered in a winter jacket, a bathing suit, or absolutely nothing.

Figure out what part of your body you're the most concerned about. Is it your stomach? Your thighs? Your ear lobes? I want you to put on an outfit that accentuates that part of yourself, but just wear it around the house. Put on a crop top, booty shorts, or put your hair in a tight ponytail and go about your business of chores, watching Netflix, and eating dinner. Schedule it for times when you're definitely alone, and then start doing it at home in front of anyone you live with. Eventually, I want you to go outside in the outfit. Just go to your mailbox, or walk your dog to the end of your driveway. Show yourself that leaving the house in something that shows your stretch marks isn't going to have any negative consequences. You don't ever have to wear that crop top out in the world for real. The point is to become comfortable with the parts of yourself that cause you distress.

I've helped several of my friends deal with their altered perceptions of their own beauty, and you can, too. Some things I've noticed that help them are complimenting parts of their personality, not their appearance. If I am complimenting a physical part of them, I either focus on something very detailed like how soft their elbow skin is or the arches in their feet, or simply tell them they look beautiful. I find that drawing attention to smaller aspects of their body reminds them of their good features, and complimenting them as a whole reminds them that the hour they spent squeezing a pimple on their cheek might not have actually been necessary.

I will give genuine advice on clothing options, if I'm asked, but I encourage everyone to wear what they want. If someone tells me they really want to wear this cute pink tank top but are worried about their armpit fat, I will tell them to put it on anyway. Honestly, just getting them out of the house wearing something they're worried about can boost their confidence because you know what usually happens? No one dies! Or sometimes they'll even get a compliment from someone while we're out, confirming that there was nothing to worry about in the first place.

Body image and body dysmporphia aren't the only reasons eating disorders begin, though. Many times, there is a co-morbidity between eating disorders and depression and/or anxiety. Remember that despite Meghan Trainor offensively saying that she "tried anorexia", eating disorders are an actual mental illness, not just an extreme diet. Research has indicated that the brain in the body of a person with anorexia or bulimia tends to have physical differences, including imbalanced neurotransmitter levels (like dopamine) and larger sections (like the orbitofrontal cortex) than the brain in a person without an eating disorder. This is just a reminder that eating disorders are real, serious, and not something you can just "try". They consume the sufferer's life.

There's more to eating disorders than just anorexia and bulimia. There are combinations of symptoms, binge-eating (without purging), and orthorexia, where the person becomes obsessed with eating foods that they consider healthy, not necessarily any food. Things like orthorexia aren't recognized in the DSM-IV (read: the psychology bible) yet, but that doesn't make them any less real.

"No one commits suicide because they want to die. Then why do they do it? Because they want to stop the pain."
– Tiffanie DeBartolo

SUICIDE

There are a lot of reasons people commit suicide. Surviving abuse or trauma, suffering from a mental illness or self-mutilation, dealing with toxic relationships or bullying creates a recipe for depression and disaster. Beginning to feel hopeless and trapped is a slippery slope that is very difficult to climb back up; it is in no way impossible, but many aren't able to move back. Ending your life seems like the only option for far too many people, and it's an absolute tragedy. I've been there, and you might be surprised by how many people have been, too.

One of the highest rates of suicide comes from the transgender population, and it's not an issue that has had enough light shed on it. There is still an incredible amount of stigma attached to people who don't identify with a heteronormative gender-specific lifestyle. Consequently, people who have a fear of coming out or who have already come out and face ridicule, torment, and abuse, deal with levels of trauma and depression I can't begin to understand.

If you are reading this, and identify with a gender different than the one you were "assigned" at birth, if you identify with both genders, or none at all, if you are transitioning, if you are bisexual, you are beautiful. If you are a person with a penis who identifies as a man, you are beautiful. If you are a person with a penis who identifies as a woman, you are beautiful. If you are pansexual, you are beautiful. We are all beautiful. We are all people. We all deserve love.

One of my favorite advocates for self love, who has been through a journey of transgender dysphoria, is Laura Jane Grace of my favorite band, Against Me! She transitioned in the public eye, and I've enjoyed watching her happiness develop as she becomes truer to the person she feels she is. She actually wrote an entire album on the struggles she dealt with called Transgender Dysphoria Blues, which I recommend to anyone, especially anyone experiencing similar struggles.

The good news is that things are slowly getting better every day. Things are in NO way where they need to be in terms of laws, regulations, and general acceptance in society, but we are improving at a turtle's pace which is better than no progress at all. Recently some establishments in my city removed the gender labels from their bathroom doors and replaced them with signs that said their restrooms were gender neutral and would not stigmatize anyone from using either room. That didn't make CNN, but it's a small win! There might be people who will yell terrible things from car windows, post despicable things on social media, and even discriminate in places of business based on someone's gender and/or sexual orientation, but there will also always be people who will welcome you into their world with open arms. Don't give up., Your fight is incredibly important. Your identity matters. Your life matters. I love you.

"A setback is a setup for a comeback." – T.D. Jakes

NON-LINEAR LIFESTYLE

Good mental health isn't a linear lifestyle. Your health doesn't look like a straight upwards arrow on a graph the way it would if you were trying to visually represent time and the Kardashian's wealth. Mental health and self love look more like a bunch of loopdeeloops bouncing up and down like a balloon deflating and flying across the room. You are going to have bad days. You are going to have amazing days. You are going to do something where you feel like you are full of confidence, declaring to the world your worth and in an instant you might feel like you've been knocked down to your knees with a rude comment or a break-up.

It's okay to get knocked down, but you have to listen to Chumbawumba and get back up again. I love myself and my body. I am confident and I am in love, but it still doesn't take much to make me cry. I cry and get blood-pressure-rising-red-faced-kinda-angry when someone says something mean to me on the internet or I get into a fight with my boyfriend. In the face of conflict or self-doubt, I can still crumble, and that's okay.

The good news is that with every blow, I learn to pick myself up a little quicker. Obviously the severity of the blow plays a huge part, but I've learned that even the shittiest of situations don't keep me feeling terrible for that long anymore. I take my time to wallow and I'm ready to go again. It's taken a lot of practice. There were days where I literally didn't get off the couch for twenty hour periods, and that includes using the bathroom. I learn every single day, and every hardship and meltdown helps me learn even more.

You aren't alone in feeling like you're moving backwards sometimes. That's human. You are moving, though. Time passes, the Earth spins, and we move. Do your best to grow as much as you can, but don't beat yourself up when you find yourself not able to handle what life threw at you that day. If you want to eat a sheet cake from a grocery store in an empty bathtub, do it. I'm not judging.

Your mental health is more important than responding to voicemails, running errands, and even going to work. Your mental health is a priority, and you need to treat it as such. Shrugging off your symptoms and swallowing your feelings is the same thing as ignoring a fight with your significant other. You end up letting things build, and eventually something explodes. Don't let your mind explode! Care for yourself every single day, even if it's hard, even if it's just for ten minutes.

In the next chapter we will take the next step in your journey of self love and explore the necessity of creative living.

5 STAYING CREATIVE

The last three chapters of this book have focused on how to establish a solid foundation for self love. If you're able to maintain a positive outlook, practice self care, and keep your mind as healthy as possible, you can begin to move on to thriving wildly.

A huge part of thriving as an individual is expressing yourself creatively. You might be thinking, "I'm not an artist!", and while I disagree with you, that's okay. Artistry is in all of us, but sometimes we let it die. Art isn't limited to fine art painters who can create an image so life-like that you can't believe it's not a photograph. Art is eloquent writing, connecting with dogs you're able to train, and building furniture from scratch. Art is cooking a delicious meal, applying gorgeous make-up, and dancing your heart out. Art is everywhere, it's indescribable and completely up for interpretation. If you are putting effort into something and letting your creativity shine, then you are creating art. If you are creating art, you are an artist.

This chapter will focus on the importance of creative living in all walks of life including fashion, hobbies, and documentation.

"Inspiration exists, but it has to find us working."
– Pablo Picasso

FINDING INSPIRATION

A big part of being (and staying) creative is finding something that inspires you. Some people wake up in the morning with a dozen new ideas for projects, without needing any external input, but I am not one of those people. We all have something wonderful inside us, but sometimes we need to be poked and prodded to get it out and noticed in the world.

The internet is an incredible tool at our disposal. We tend to use it to refresh our newsfeeds to find out who is on vacation where, and which girl we went to high school with has most recently announced that she's pregnant, but that's pretty dumb. Don't get me wrong, I do that, too, but there's approximately a bajillion websites out there that can educate you and inspire you till you feel like you're about to burst.

You don't need to have ten thousand followers on social media or be active on those sites every day to get what you need from them, either. You can make a profile on Pinterest or Instagram and get lost in the depths of ideas for hours without ever gaining a follower. You always have the option to make your information private and accessible only to you, if being in the public eye in any capacity is a deterrent for you.

As great as the internet is, though, there are many other sources to draw ideas from. Thousands of brilliant ideas were created before Al Gore, or whoever it was, shot up in bed in the middle of the night and said, "I'm going to create the internet." The best way I know to get inspired is to get out of my house. Most of the time, when I'm at a loss for ideas, I will look around where I am and observe. If I'm always in my bedroom, the things I see are going to be pretty limited. Yeah, I do my best to make my living space a fun environment, but I can only look at the same plastic balloons, tinsel garlands, and DVD sets for so long before I'm out of ideas. Leave the house.

If you live in a city, you can tumble out your doorstep into an environment of chaos; colorful buildings, crazy people having fights on the street, absurd objects left on the ground. You can find an infinite amount of inspiration from being in a city just for a few hours. Sit on a bench and people watch, ride public transportation, speak to people near you. You can create a game before you leave the house where you have to find certain scenarios before you go home. You could play People Watch Bingo, try to eat a new cuisine on every outing you take, explore alleys, and stop to say hi to dogs on walks. Don't be afraid to turn around and go back to something that caught your eye.

If you live in the country, you can venture into the outdoors and breathe in the beauty of nature. Look for patterns in tree bark, investigate shadows, and figure out which way the birds are traveling. Sit on a hill letting the breeze hit your face, stick your feet in a creek, and collect pine cones, shells, and stones that speak to you. Let the stillness surround you and listen to the thoughts in your head.

Even if you live in a suburb, you can apply these concepts to people-watching, collecting, and wandering. You can also make a point to take trips to the city and country, as it interests you. The idea is to pay attention to your five senses. Always stop and take stock of what you're physically experiencing at any given moment. Do you hear a siren from a mile away? Can you tell if it's from a police car, ambulance, or fire truck? Do you smell pollen but can't see any flowers? Follow your nose till you find a meadow. Drawing attention to your senses is a great way to practice mindfulness, and being mindful makes it easier to be creative.

Besides your surroundings and the internet, another way to find inspiration is to try something new. Scratch something off your bucket list or teach someone else how to do something. New experiences make you think about things you haven't yet, or at least in a new way. Making your mind function differently is key to getting your creative juices flowing. I love doing that by asking questions like, "What is your least favorite superhero, vegetable, or band?" You end up making your brain work "backwards", almost, and you can become more heightened and aware in that moment, more receptive to new ideas.

Other people are another huge source of inspiration. Surrounding yourself with people who are fabulous and go-getters is going to make you want to do more! Remember, if you're jealous of something, that's a call to action to go out and get what you want! Hang out with people who have things that you want for a day, or live life in a way you'd be happy to emulate and I bet you when you get home you'll have a lot of energy. You might find yourself diving into a new project, organizing your supplies, or just making a to do list. This is all progress.

CREATIVE SPACE

As an artist, you need a space to create. Not everyone can have a studio in a separate building, or an entire room in their house dedicated to their craft. However, you do need to designate an area to the art you are passionate about expressing. That might mean prioritizing space in your bedroom for a craft caddy, spending a lot of energy organizing your pantry and kitchen tools, or organizing your closet in a way that allows you to see everything you have to wear and create the most bad-ass traffic-stopping outfits of all time.

As I've said before, we are all artists, but our art is very different. What do you need to be successful with your art? Is it a flat surface, comfortable chair, and gel point pens to write your manuscript? Is it a bag that organizes all your photography equipment so you can take it all out to a shoot at a moment's notice? Take care of your supplies and give them priority in your life.

Having a space that you dedicate to your passion is important, and signifies commitment. It's definitely possible to do everything you do from your couch while re-watching Friends DVDs, but when you make the decision to move over to that section of your room or go into the studio and close the door, you're more likely to be serious about your work at that time and really concentrate and create quality work.

This also means respecting your work environment. Wash the dishes when you're done cooking, clean out your paint brushes so they don't harden, and throw away trash after you've finished an installation. Take pride in your space, indicating that you take pride in your art. If (when) your art ever takes off, you'll have a great practice in place of treating space with respect, and it will translate over to potential clients you'll work with. They'll think you're more professional with a clean work space than a cluttered, dirty one.

Creating in a clean space also promotes creativity. When my desk is so cluttered I can't see the bottom of it, I feel super anxious and just put off working. Once I clean everything up and organize my materials, I become inspired to work! Yeah, creative minds are often cluttered, but I'd say that most of us work at our highest potential when we can see the supplies we have access to and have a clean, convenient space to work.

Cleaning your space can apply to your head space, too. If you're preoccupied by a flooded inbox or a fight you're having with your best friend, you might not be able to make your best product. Before you sit down to work, make sure that you've tied up as many loose ends as possible, so you can be focused and productive! One hour of pure concentration and deliberation is more efficient than three hours of scattered progress and wandering thoughts.

"Fashion is chaotic, and it can be an aggravation, too, but it is at its best when it allows you to express yourself."
– John Malkovich

FASHION

It's no secret that expressing yourself with clothing is fun and a very tangible way to create a message. We're visual creatures, so whether you realize it or not you're sending a signal to people around you just by what you're wearing. The most nonjudgmental, accepting person will immediately create a different thought about two people next to each other, one wearing a pink polo shirt with a popped collar, khaki shorts, flamingo printed belt, and tan moccasins and the other in baggy black pants with a silver chain connected to a wallet, black satin corset, and velvet choker necklace. We make snap decisions about people as a species, and that can inform their decision about interacting with you. Now, you should be able to be kind and communicative to anyone who approaches you regardless of their clothing. The same person can wear sweatpants on Monday, an evening gown on Tuesday, and a plaid school-girl outfit on Wednesday, so it's not fair to say you couldn't be friends with someone based on their outfit. My point is, dressing in a way that reflects how you feel and what you want to attract can have a lot of benefits.

Everyone has the option to be fashionable. Fashion has become a big part of our culture, and there's a large level of importance attached to it. The industry makes more money than most will ever even be able to comprehend, but that doesn't mean you have to listen to it. You don't have to conform to what you are being told. What colors, cuts, and prints are "hot" this season doesn't need to be on your radar if you decide they're not important.

Just because you're not following trends like a religion doesn't mean you can't be fashionable, though. To me, being fashionable is not synonymous with being trendy. Wear what you want, always. When I talked about loving your body, I reminded you that you don't need to dress for your body type. Remember that! You can wear whatever you want at any size, inspired by any decade, in any color. I think the most interesting fashion icons have completely ignored what's in style, and just done their own thing their whole lives.

Finding your style is a constantly evolving thing. I don't know anyone who hasn't gone through phases in their wardrobes. When I was a teenager, I wore jeans with holes in them, a white studded belt buckled on the hip, children's sized band T-shirts, dozens of plastic bracelets, and Chuck Taylors with mismatched socks. As a child, I wore red stirrup leggings and a men's sized XL T-shirt that came with our vacuum. It said "Dirt Devil, Paint The Town Red" and I wore it as a dress. The important thing is, at each of those times, I thought I looked good and the clothes I put on my body reflected how I felt and wanted to feel.

Right now, my style is pretty much colorful dresses with colorful tights and/or leggings, ballet flats, and possibly a cardigan or shrug on top. I don't really change my look to match the seasons. I wear floral prints and neon sandals year-round. I'm never concerned with matching patterns or overdoing it on bright colors.

There are times I wish I could have a more severe look. Sometimes I wish I could wear black mesh tops, skin tight black jeans, bold jewelry, and chic hair-dos. Or wear flowy white skirts and have braids in my hair, channeling the hippies at Woodstock. First of all, I can have all those things. If I choose to dress that way one day out of the week without warning or transition, I can, without anyone's permission, so I know that it doesn't need to be a "wish". What I mean is that my comfortable and natural state is simple dresses and leggings with comfy shoes. I want everything to be colorful and sparkly, but that's really all I care about. At the end of the day, that's my style and I'm okay with it! Your current, past, and future styles are all acceptable and awesome. Fashion and style is ever-evolving and you can try out as many things as your heart desires, but if you feel comfortable in something that people don't agree is up to snuff, then fuck 'em. You should only ever dress for yourself.

I also include beauty regiments. I would much rather prioritize my time running errands, making art, and hanging out with my friends than spending ninety minutes on my hair. Do I know that I could make my hair look bangin' if I spent that much time on it every day?

Yeah I do, but my priorities just aren't there. If what makes you the happiest and feel the most beautiful is an in-depth make-up regime, then make time for it (like we talked about in Self Care). If you don't prefer to spend time and money on getting your hair dyed, styled, having fancy make-up, or "On Fleek" eyebrows, it's totally cool, too. I support that. I'd rather live my life out loud in the world with no mascara than stay in, sheltered, with luscious lashes.

I grew up watching shows that would go into women's homes, telling them how terrible their closets and clothing choices were. They would make them feel terrible about how they had been dressing for years and take them on a shopping spree at fancy stores with thousands of dollars, but they'd only be able to buy a few pieces because the prices were so high. They'd get a professional stylist to "fix" their hair, wax their eyebrows, and put make-up on their face. At the end of the show, they'd strut down onto the stage as the audience clapped, applauding their transformation.

Here's the thing, though: I can't remember one example from these shows where the reason that these women were dressing "frumpy" wasn't because they had low self-esteem or were so over-worked that they didn't have time to put hours of effort into their external appearance. I believe that if these shows had put more resources into working on these women's self worth, they would have eventually started dressing in a way that made them happier or feel more beautiful. Or they wouldn't! Maybe 90's Tweety bird sweatshirts are awesome in that lady's eyes. If you want to wear a bedazzled cartoon sweatshirt that is older than your children, go ahead. It's seriously fine.

Fashion is fun. It's amazing to experiment with new looks and find out what you feel the best in, but there's more to life. Self love and care are the most important parts that you need to figure out first, and once you have those, fashion will fall into place. You can wear a designer dress more expensive than my house, but if you're uncomfortable in it, you're not going to radiate like you could. Confidence is the sexiest accessory, for real.

"A hobby a day keeps the doldrums away."
– Phyllis McGinley

HOBBIES

Having a hobby isn't always easy. In high school I went to school, danced three hours after the last period, and went home to do homework and hang out with my friends. There were other things I enjoyed doing, but I didn't have much time so they were always after thoughts. I would write ten page notes to my best friend that I'd decorate with magazine clippings and quotes, send letters to my friends I'd see the next day, and had shoe boxes full of sparkly craft supplies, but I didn't really have anything formed as far as interests beyond dancing.

After high school, I suddenly had all this extra time and realized I didn't have ways to occupy my time alone. My boyfriend would get really frustrated with me because I always wanted to spend my free time with him. He told me, not so gently, that I needed to get some hobbies of my own. He knew I liked sending mail, even though it was just little "thinking of you" notes I'd send to my real-life friends, so he went on the internet and found Postcrossing. That was the beginning.

Postcrossing was a site that facilitated international exchanges of postcards. I became obsessed with it and sent about 1,500 postcards through that site. In the process, I found Swap-Bot, a similar site that facilitated postal exchanges, but for more than just postcards. I found a bunch of pen pals and got goodies from all over the world. I still talk to a few people I met on these sites. I began hoarding all these supplies and realized all I was doing was getting more things to create with but not actually making. My boyfriend nudged me again to start creating stuff.

I joined Mail Art 365, a challenge to send a piece of mail art every day for a whole year. It was quite a task, but I can't tell you how beneficial it was. I set up rules for myself, like I was allowed to work in chunks (i.e. not literally making one piece every morning, seven at a time was fine). I met a ton of creative people in the community, developing not only my artistic skills but dedication and organizational skills I would continue to use for the rest of my life.

Finishing that project gave me an enormous source of pride. It also got me through one of the toughest years of my life with trying out a dozen different medications, going through CBT, and dealing with my grandmother's death. I'm not sure how I would have handled those things if I hadn't had that creative outlet.

Opening up my mind to mail made it easier for me to dabble in other mediums, such as blogging, journaling, and performance art. More importantly, I discovered street art, which is one of my biggest passions. You might not like mail like I do, and that's fine. Most people don't! I still love mail, but it's not my biggest creative go-to anymore. My point is that mail was an amazing starting point for me that allowed me to branch off not only creatively, but build up contacts in my world.

In my late twenties, I still know people who struggle with finding hobbies. If you can identify with this, don't worry. First of all, it's never too late to try something new. You might not like everything you try, but you won't know it till you go for it. If you have even a slight interest, it's worth exploring. I had always wanted to know how juggle, but it seemed impossible. One night, my friend invited me to meet him at a church in the city for a "meet up", and I had no idea what was going on. I went because I like surprises, and it turned out to be fantastic. That "meet up" was called Independent Circus Practice. I walked in. There were pairs of people juggling everything from pins to discs, tall men walking across tight ropes, and women perched in position on top of their partner in aerial yoga moves. There were trapeze artists, wrapped up in aerial fabric, hula hoopers, fire eaters. It was beautiful and overwhelming. My friend began teaching me to juggle and I sucked so bad at first. He had me start with just one ball and it seemed pointless to me. He told me to catch that ball one hundred times in a row before I moved onto two balls, It seemed like such a waste of time, but I listened.

I came back every Monday night for a couple months. I graduated to two balls, then three. I still remember the first time I was able to actually catch all three balls. Even though it was only one round, I was immediately ecstatic. My mouth opened in shock like Tom Haverford in *Parks And Recreation* when he sees Jerry do something dumb. I was so happy it happened, but I eventually stopped going because it wasn't something I was incredibly passionate about. You don't have to follow through on everything you try.

Trying new things is terrifying and exciting, but it can yield a lot of great results. At the very least, you might make a new friend, and that's an amazing thing. Making an effort is rewarding, and having skills up your sleeve will eventually prove useful. Really, though, the more hobbies and interests you develop, the easier it will be for you to be alone with yourself. You'll begin having more fun with yourself and not need the company of others to be happy, if that's something you're struggling with. (Or you'll meet more people and have more options of friends to spend time with!)

"Creativity is seeing what everyone else has seen, and thinking what no one else has thought." – Albert Einstein

EVERYDAY ACTIVITIES

Being creative doesn't need to be limited to a canvas or during the time you allot for your hobbies. Days can be much happier and fulfilling if you try to incorporate your creative mind into the chores and errands you've previously labeled as mundane. Putting dishes in the dishwasher, folding clean laundry, and going grocery shopping aren't most people's jams. It can be pretty boring if you don't try to liven it up. The good news is you can liven up anything with minimal effort.

The first step is to add music to whatever you're doing. I've only met two people in my life that actively dislike music who are blessed enough to be able to physically hear it. Music is something that has a strong effect on pretty much everyone, but obviously the kind of music makes a difference. Our reactions to Skid Row and Taylor Swift are probably drastically different, so putting effort into what we're listening to is important. Make playlists often, explore new bands on a regular basis, and make sure you're pressing play before you start your to do list.

I find that listening to the radio is a passive experience. Not only are you not in control of what you're hearing, but you also have to deal with commercials and DJ banter. If you have the luxury of a smart phone, MP3 player, or laptop, you have access to things like Spotify, Pandora Radio, and iTunes for free. Use them! Listen to music you love and things you might learn to love instead of the same Top 40 songs on repeat. Whether you love pop music or not, things get overplayed easily.

After you've made sure that you're utilizing music as often as possible to make your experiences more enjoyable, try to think out of the box. Lists are a great tool in this stage. One time, I made a list of 100 Ways To Use A Pencil. It seems impossible to list that many things to use a small stick that we know as a writing utensil, but I did it. Some of them are extremely unconventional. Some of them are downright absurd, but life doesn't need to be basic and conforming.

Figure out activities you have to do that you don't find particularly fun, and brainstorm ways to make them a little more interesting. You could organize your grocery cart by color as you add items to it, channel a celebrity as you're getting dressed, or take on an accent as you dispute your cable bill over the phone. Fold your towels the way they do in honeymoon suites, make faces in your food, and use novelty supplies as normal ones—that fancy watering can doesn't need to be display. Use it to—wait for it—water your plants!

Nothing you do needs to be boring. If you wake up, hankering for spaghetti, make some for breakfast. If you want to wear rain boots when the forecast is for clear skies, plan your outfit accordingly. Blow bubbles out the passenger's side window as your friend drives you to dinner, bring party hats to board game night, collect things you find on the street while you walk to your car in the morning and create a sculpture with them. The world is full of shit to make things with, so use it.

A surefire way to reignite your passion for the world and all it has to offer is to turn off your laptop, phone, and general communicative technology for a day or so. It can be really difficult to shut out something that you're so used to using—we've all become pretty dependent on our phones at the very least. Schedule out a day (and tell your friends in advance you might be unreachable) to go out in the world and not worry about updating social media, responding to texts, or hearing the notifications as you get a new e-mail. I've done experiments with taking out all technology—including television, radio, GPS, etc. and that's been even more difficult because you can't control your surroundings, but it's been a really worthwhile experience. Honestly, even ten hours is beneficial. Try it!

Since my job is blogging, ruling out the internet can actually affect my job, but if your job involves massive amounts of time staring at a screen, it becomes even more imperative to remove yourself from that environment as often as possible.

"Kindness in words creates confidence. Kindness in thinking creates profoundness. Kindness in giving creates love."
– Lao Tzu

RANDOM ACTS OF KINDNESS

Starting guerrilla art was a huge turning point in my life because I realized that I could simultaneously be creative, share my work, and potentially make someone else happy. The idea that you're walking down the street and see something bright and gorgeous might prompt you to think about the time that someone spent making it. You might feel a connection to the piece, you might not, but you definitely stopped and saw it. Sometimes that's enough, just to get the person out of their auto-pilot drone zone.

Making art and putting it on the street might not be your thing (although you won't know till you try), but the idea behind a random act of kindness is something I think you should pay attention to.

Random acts of kindness may or may not be as pre-meditated as measuring a pole, knitting a piece, and sewing it on for people to see, but it can have the same effect. Every single day, the people you pass and interact with in the world are dealing with something. We all have stress and sorrow. The person you see at the bank today might be having one of the worst days they can ever remember. You never know when you could be the turning point in someone's day or life. You have the constant opportunity to be someone's restoration of faith in humanity, so act as though every interaction you have with someone could be that moment.

Kindness is simple. It can be as easy as smiling at someone, giving a genuine compliment, or helping someone pick up things they dropped. Being aware and considerate of how you're affecting other people and their lives is a huge step in kindness. Do you have a shopping cart full of stuff and the person behind you in line is just holding a box of tissues and a DVD? You can let them go in front of you in line. They might protest, but they might thank you profusely. That might be the one thing that makes their day. Putting other people in a good mood benefits you eventually. Even if the person you're giving a gift or service doesn't give you something in return, they are more likely to go out and do something nice for a stranger. If everyone was constantly doing nice things for everyone else, we would be in a perpetual state of positive energy and you would reap the benefits as much as you would deliver them.

HERE'S A LIST OF 100 RANDOM ACTS OF KINDNESS

Genuinely compliment strangers

Buy the person's food behind you in the drive-thru

Add googly eyes to a friend's mailbox

Volunteer

Make art and abandon it for someone to find

Print out happy photos and pin them on community bulletin boards

Figure out how to reduce your carbon footprint

Pay off someone's layaway

Remind an adult how to be a kid

Send a letter or note in the mail

Pass out flowers

Donate to a charity

Give a meal, money, or supplies to a homeless person

Post funny videos on your friend's Facebook

Leave notes on windshields

Put change in parking meters that are out of time

Only say positive and constructive things online

Bring your friend an energy drink at work

Be careful not to splash pedestrians with puddles while driving on rainy days

Let your loved ones know they are beautiful

Teach someone something

Pick up things you accidentally knock over in stores

Recycle

Gift a scratch off lottery ticket

Leave quarters in toy vending machines

Let someone in line in front of you

Hold the door open for someone

Come up with a list of TV shows, movies, books, bands, or comics that a friend might enjoy

Pull off elaborate and nice pranks

Write nice messages with sidewalk chalk

Tape money to a soda machine for the next person to use

Grant a wish within your power

Help a neighbor with yard work or cooking

Leave papers with quotes or sayings in books at stores

Go to events that are important to friends, even if they aren't your cup of tea

Help someone practice for an interview

Watch someone's house, kids, or pets for free

Bring in some snacks for coworkers

Be kind and make eye contact with cashiers, toll booth operators, etc.

Leave notes on mirrors

Pick up litter

Write a note of recommendation

Draw and write fun things on mirrors with dry erase markers

Bring drinks and treats to your local post office or fire station

Plant trees and flowers (especially in places that could use some life and color)

Don't judge or discriminate

Help someone pick up things they've dropped – Symbolically 'adopt' an animal

Make mix CDs for friends or leave them for strangers

Fill flash drives with beautiful pictures and fun music and leave it somewhere

Send flowers to someone at their job

Donate clothes to a thrift store

Buy someone a drink from across the bar

Make a bird feeder for your yard

• **100** •

CIRCLE FIVE YOU WANT TO TRY THIS MONTH

Adopt your pet from a shelter

Leave a nice note in the copier or fax machine at work

Hold a fundraiser for someone else or a charity

Pay attention to people in person instead of playing on your phone

Always get a doggy bag at a restaurant for leftovers to give to a homeless person

Wrap up books and write clues as to what the book is about before you leave them somewhere

Leave excellent tips

Give someone a second chance

Call a family member who always wants to hear from you

Set up single friends

Put the cart back when you're done shopping

Write something sweet on your friend's back windshield with a window marker

Put out a bowl of candy on your desk for coworkers

Offer to be the designated driver

Bake a cake for no reason and write something silly in icing

Do something really weird, to give a stranger a story to tell

Offer to go get the car while your friends wait when it's raining

Promote your friends' work

Give thoughtful gifts for non birthday/Christmas reasons

If you have extra time on your parking slip, pass it to the person pulling in after you

Leave face-up pennies on the ground to grant others good luck

Apologize in person

Include friends you might not usually

Decorate your house for others to enjoy

Offer to take someone's shift who needs the day off

Do a guerrilla art installation for others to smile at or interact with

Show someone around town who just moved there

Return favors

Write a long list of reasons you love your significant other or friend

Keep supplies on you for others to use (pens, gum, tampons)

Intervene if someone needs help

Be positive, offer encouragement and support

Take care of something for your friend who really didn't want to do it themselves

Give good hugs

Donate blood

Give helpful advice to someone new at work

Leave little reminders around town

Lend someone money

Pack someone a lunch

Offer a foot, hand, shoulder massage

Instead of making a gift wish list, ask people to donate to a charity or do a RAOK and tell you about it

Slip a dollar in the DVD case at the Redbox for the next person

Every time you say something negative, put a dollar in a jar and use the money to buy someone else something nice

Give helpful advice to someone new at work

Hold up a sign saying 'Have a great day!' on the side of the road

Pass out candy to people waiting at the DMV

Buy your pet a special treat

Make Easter baskets for kids in the hospital

Mail a care package

"Life moves so fast. You gotta document the good times, man."
– Big Boi

DOCUMENTATION

I'm obsessed with documenting things. I have my text messages set to save as many as it can before it starts deleting them, I have an app in my phone that lets me write down notes, ideas, and things to do later. I share photos from my phone on Instagram. I have journals dedicated to specific things like happy thoughts, self love journaling, and quotes I collect. I take pictures of as much as I possibly can, and bring my DSLR and phone with me everywhere I go in case an opportunity to visually document something presents itself. I have paper and pen on me at all times, too. I write my thoughts on my blog, I keep a running bucket list for life goals, and I save important tangible mementos in boxes.

There's actually more that I do, but you get the idea. Not everyone likes documenting the way I do, and that's fine. I think we can agree that's a bit overboard, but I think that documenting your life is a very important thing, especially the good things.

Since I'm a huge advocate for keeping a Happy Journal, I have many friends who try it out for themselves and tell me their experiences. Their feedback has been overwhelmingly positive, but one testimonial really stood out to me. She told me she realized her whole life she'd only gone to write in her journal when she was sad, filling up books with negative, self deprecating, sad thoughts. Now she was doing the exact opposite and realized how beneficial it was.

Think about it, when you were a teenager if you kept a journal it was probably pretty angsty. I kept journals all throughout my school years, starting as early as eight-years-old. I tended to only write in the journals when something bad was happening. Now, don't get me wrong, journaling is an amazing tool to use to figure out feelings. I've learned a lot about myself and the problems I was experiencing by writing them down, but what ends up happening is you have this journal full of negative thoughts. I had this really cool notebook I bought at Hot Topic with Edward Scissorhands on the front, and all I wrote in it was how much I hated myself, my problems with my parents, and issues with boys. There was physical blood smeared in there from nights I had hurt myself, and distorted words from where tears had landed on the ink.

I never got rid of that book, because it definitely did help me at that time. Through moves and decluttering sessions, I've never been able to toss it, but I've also never been able to open it to read the words again. It served its purpose at the time, but now all I have is this very tangible reminder of shitty feelings.

When I hold one of my completed Happy Journals (and by completed, I mean I ran out of pages), I get a very different feeling. I feel gratitude, hope, and joy. I know that in the days I've documented there were tears, panic attacks, and break-ups. I know there was a ton of pain in between the lines, but what I chose to write was "Making up with ____" on August 10th instead of a drawn out rant about the fight that I had with him on August 9th. I chose to focus on the good inside that book, which makes me feel good.

There's always going to be pain. I can't fix that for you. I can't stop cancer, divorce, and mental illness. I can just give you tools to help deal with and overcome these issues. Documenting everything is important, and I think it's a great idea to create evidence of the life you've lived. You never know, it might inspire someone some day. And if your journal ends up helping one person, it's done more than its job.

You might prefer to spend an equal amount of energy documenting pain and joy, or more on the former. It's up to you, always. The thing is, you can only document with great precision for finite periods of time. I'm not telling you to walk around with a camera dangling from your neck, viewing life through a lens, but if you want to capture a photo you only have a second to do it. Writing gives you a little more time to record an event or feelings, but doing it as close to the time it happened has an incredible benefit. I honestly can't even tell you the details of how my first relationship ended because it was so long ago that I don't remember. Stories become faded and confused, and sometimes the only way to have the truth is to read what you wrote down in the moment.

If you don't want to document things, that's fine. You can live in the moment and be as minimalistic as you'd like. All advice is disposable. I just know that people love looking at old photos, reading quotes they wrote down from nights their best friend got super wasted, and reading what life was like.

In the next chapter we will focus on how to interact and connect with other people who will support us to learn about life and progress in our journey of self love.

THINGS TO TRY:

- Keep a list of quotes you hear from inspiring people or funny things your friends say
- Make your living space beautiful
- Unplug from the internet and/or your phone
- Pour glitter, confetti, or sequins all over yourself
- Put a disposable camera and journal in your car for your friends to use
- Have a crafternoon
- Decorate your refrigerator
- Dye your hair
- Stargaze
- Complete an online tutorial you've bookmarked for later
- Mix patterns that people say clash
- Decorate cupcakes
- Explore strange roadside attractions
- Try to change your handwriting for the length of an entire letter
- Start a blog
- Create your own mandala, or color one in
- Recreate a photo you think is beautiful
- Choreograph a dance
- Design your own flag
- Leave twinkle lights up year round
- Decorate for every holiday
- Wrap every item of a present individually
- Have an art picnic
- Throw an unbirthday party
- Decorate the inside of your car
- Incorporate every color of the rainbow into your outfit
- Document the moon for an entire cycle and how you feel daily
- Build a fort

- Used colored staples and fancy office supplies
- Document your week in paper scraps
- Leave anonymous notes for strangers
- Play the cloud game
- Make paper snowflakes out of colored paper
- Draw with sidewalk chalk
- Bedazzle something
- Make a natural mandala or artwork sculpture with flowers, rocks, shells, etc.
- Take a road trip to somewhere within 90 minutes to somewhere you've never been before
- Make your own artistamps (fake postage)
- Communicate with someone via text but only with images, no words
- Make a mix CD
- Take a picture in the same spot every day for a week
- Turn off the TV and listen to music instead
- Melt crayons on something
- Play dress up
- Reorganize your workspace
- Decorate a bus stop shelter
- Build a time capsule to open later
- Hold a bubble gun while you ride around on your bike
- Run through a sprinkler
- Learn how to juggle
- Make your own sushi
- Build a terrarium
- Dance on top of bubble wrap
- Figure out what your life story is (so far) in just six words
- Make a blackout poem
- Plan an elaborate scavenger hunt

6 CONNECTING

Loving yourself happens first, but once you've created a solid foundation, you can truly enhance your life with the presence of the right kind of people. Finding people who inspire you and make you want to reach your highest potential is a great way to encourage yourself along in life. In this chapter, I'll go over ways to find friends, network, strengthen existing relationships, and weed out the people you don't need in your life.

This chapter will hone in on the importance of creating all types of relationships to expand your opportunities, support system, and personal growth.

"I like to connect with people in the virtual world, exchanging thought and ideas, when in the physical world we might never have the opportunity to cross paths." – Demi Moore

USING THE INTERNET

I mentioned that the internet is a great tool for inspiration, but it's bigger than just learning how to make your birthday party look like it came out of a design book or finding ideas for your next big project. One of the most fabulous things about the internet is its ability to connect people. Before the internet, if you had different interests to your peers, you were labeled as a Weirdo. Now, while there might not be a group of kids at school who share your love of metal music or Tarot cards, you can reach out online and develop relationships with people who totally get you. They might be far away, but you might feel more comforted knowing you're not alone.

Figuring out what your interests and hobbies are is a great way to establish friends online. If you like doing something, there's probably a group about it online! You can find lots of social media communities just by doing a general keyword search. You'd think snail mail is a bit of a niche hobby, but there are dozens and dozens of groups and websites dedicated to the subject online. It doesn't take long to find people interested in the same things as you.

There was a point in my life when I felt the only people I connected with were online, though, and it kind of sucked. Sure, I texted and e-mailed them every day to share pictures, stories, and philosophies but it wasn't the same as doing it in person. I felt like knowing that there were people out there who got me but I couldn't connect with in-person was almost worse than wondering if anyone out there understood me at all.

I recommend seeking out both online and "real life" relationships with people in close proximity to you. I get something different from all of my "real life" friends; some of them are amazing at adventuring and getting into strange shenanigans, some are great listeners and help with figuring out conflicts and brainstorming theories on life, and some are incredibly creative and inspire me to get my butt in gear. It's okay to get things from online friends that you don't get from your friends in person, but it's important to try to find people you can connect with near where you live as well.

"Everyone should build their network before they need it."
– Dave Delaney

NETWORKING

There are in-person opportunities for meeting like-minded people the same way there are communities online based on common interests. These are a little more difficult to find, and it might involve a bit of travel, but they're out there and they're worth it. I've been to socials, meet-ups, conferences, and workshops focused around very specific ideas. People will meet up to write letters, play card games, and brainstorm solutions for issues in your city.

If you're in a less populated area, you might have to do a bit of traveling occasionally. Cities are obviously filled with more people, classrooms, and venues but I've found plenty of knitting groups, writing workshops, and art classes in the suburbs. If you have the means to travel to a place that's got something you want, make it a priority. You don't have to go to their meetings every week! Just once every other month is better than nothing, especially if you use that time to socialize your butt off.

Socializing might seem really intimidating at first. I'm a very extroverted person, and it's still awkward for me at first. When I go to larger conferences I feel like such a little fish and start questioning whether I even have what it takes to be there! I get shy (I know that's hard to believe) and want to just sit in my seat, writing down the information delivered in the lectures.

One of the biggest motivators for me to initiate conversations with people I don't know at these functions is networking and my business. I know that introducing myself to people with similar interests isn't just good for my personal and social life, it's hugely beneficial to my business. You might not have a business you're trying to get "more eyes on", but if your goal is to get more friends and contacts, you have to assume you'll be the one who needs to make the first move.

I've found a really good way to make this awkward thing easier is to offer a gift. When I go to conferences and larger workshops, I spend a couple hours beforehand making little packets for the people I meet. It sounds way more complicated than it is. I'll just get miniature treat sacks (the size of your palm) and slide in my business card, a sticker, and one other thing like a trading card, fortune, or temporary tattoo. Business cards fly around these events like birds that just realized it's time to head south, so it's really nice to have something that looks like a bigger deal than everyone else's offering.

The cost of the treat sacks and stickers is minimal compared to how many people remember me as a result of them. Also, going up to a stranger with something sealed that looks like it's for them specifically is a very easy "in" to striking up a conversation. You always want to shake hands, repeat their name, and smile. Ask them at least one question about themselves, demonstrate your interest, and ask for their business card. Not everyone you meet is going to be your new best friend, but you never know who you might connect with or who could help you out (or vice versa) in the future.

After you meet someone new, I find it's a really good practice to follow up with them. Add them on social media, since you have their information now, and send them a short and sweet message. Use their first name, say how good it was to meet them, and ask if there's any way you can support them. That can be as simple as "liking" their Facebook page or sharing a link of their band's new album on your Twitter feed. If you had an inside joke or remember something specific about them, throw it in casually to let them know you remember them!

"Letters are something from you. It's a different kind of intention than writing an e-mail." – Keanu Reeves

SNAIL MAIL

Yes, snail mail is a super cool hobby that I think you might enjoy. I know I preach about it a lot, but I'm not going to urge you to get fifty pen pals if that's not something you can imagine yourself doing! I just want to make a note about the personal touch that snail mail has and how it can be a huge help in obtaining contacts, maintaining relationships, and reaching out to your audience for help.

In this hyper-technological age, e-mails can become a huge burden. An inbox bursting at the seams feels daunting and dreadful, whereas getting something handwritten in the mailbox (among bills and junk mail catalogs) can completely make someone's day. Sending something in the mail is a big deal nowadays because it demonstrates a personal touch that most people fail to give things anymore.

You can use snail mail as a tool to reach out to people you've met or worked with and say thank you for their time. It doesn't need to be elaborate, just a few sentences is amazing! Thank you notes are also great for a potential employer who just interviewed you, or your aunt who sent you a check for your birthday. You can make baller invitations to let people know about a party you're throwing. They'll probably be more intrigued about coming than if they read your Facebook invite which got lost under the other twenty invites they were sent that day. You can strengthen your business and contacts by sending out newsletters, coupons, and announcements that will benefit the recipient, and you can learn more about people you meet in online groups by exchanging handwritten letters with them.

Don't forget to use snail mail to your advantage. It's pretty amazing. You can put a dollar's worth of postage on an envelope, give it to a postal employee and say, "Hey, can you take this to Australia for me?" and they do it. Sure, postage adds up, but mail is a beautiful institution that should be maintained!

"Your vibe attracts your tribe." – Unknown

MAKING FRIENDS

Making friends as an adult can feel really uncomfortable and strange. While it's not easy for everyone in high school to make friends, it's a lot easier to do so in that environment than as an adult in the real world. It's the same with finding people to date.

In high school and college you met people in classes and at social events, realized you had something in common, and saw each other later that week at the same class or event. It was easy to keep up your relationship because they were automatically scheduled into your life! They had to be in Economics 201 the same time you did, so things were simple. When you graduate, you have to evaluate if you want to make time for that person on your own terms, and it turns out we usually don't.

Making friends as an adult can suck. You can feel vulnerable, awkward, and needy all at once, but you don't need to. There are tons of people who want more friends in their life, and even more who wouldn't say no to a new friend even if they feel satisfied with their current social circle.

With the exception of the internet, it can be pretty difficult to make friends just staying in your house. If you're unsatisfied with any aspect of your life, it won't get better on its own. Not only do you have to put in work, but if you're doing the same thing over and over without the results you want, you are going to have to revisit the way you're approaching the problem. So even if you're really nervous about going to a social event to meet new friends, know that staying in your house isn't going to yield groundbreaking results.

If one of your friends was complaining that they didn't have a boyfriend, but all they did was stay in their house all day and didn't even have an online dating profile, you'd probably tell them they needed to do more to get what they wanted, right? Give yourself the same advice.

When you're out in the world, no one is going to assume you want to be their friend. In America, social norms teach us to give ample personal space and to generally keep to ourselves in public. If you want to meet someone, you have to invite them into your space. It can be really simple, though. Smiling, complimenting something they're wearing, or making a funny comment about something that's happening around both of you at that moment are great ice breakers that will make that person realize you are at least interested in having a conversation with them.

You aren't going to have an instant connection with everyone, and you might even end up severely disliking someone you start talking to. That's okay! Keep your head up and move on to the next person. If one or both of you aren't feeling it, it won't be a relationship worth pursuing.

When you choose to have someone in your life because they bring you joy, you need to make an effort to keep in touch with them. Everyone has different preferences for communication, and sometimes you'll need to compromise your ideals to maintain a friendship. The good news is there are tons of options for communicating with your friends these days. So as long as you're both on board with how you're talking, it can be via text, Skype, e-mail, phone calls, instant messages, Facebook, or whatever else you decide.

It's also okay to have different types of friends. You might have someone you exchange letters with every few months, someone you have a scheduled one hour phone call with every week, and someone you text every waking thought to. You can have friends you only talk about a specific hobby with, friends you go on adventures with, and friends you spill your soul to. Figure out what you want most in your life, and try to find it.

"There are so many different walks of life, so many different personalities in the world. And no longer do you have to be a chameleon and try and adapt to that environment - you can truly be yourself." – Hope Solo

PERSONALITY TESTS

Tests like Myers-Briggs Personality Test and Enneagram Personality Type are fascinating tools. After just thirty or forty questions, these tests can pinpoint things about you such as interests, strengths, compatibility levels with romantic partners, and what you're more likely to be addicted to.

There are a lot of variables to consider when taking one of these tests and reading the results. These tests potentially imply that there are only 10-16 types of people in the world, and you must fall into one of those categories. You're obviously incredibly unique and I bet you can think of more than sixteen types of people you've met in your life. The idea, though, is that there are formulas and consistencies in the way we think and behave that can make things like finding a friend or significant other much easier.

Myers-Briggs has four sections, and you're one of two things for each section - Extroverted/Introverted, Intuitive/Sensing, Thinking/Feeling, Judging/Perceiving. I am an ENFP that can easily flip-flop over to an ESFP. This personality test says that I am warm, enthusiastic, and passionate. It says I'm a generally happy risk-taking person that thrives in a flexible environment. That's pretty spot on.

The Enneagram Personality Type says that I am a 7 or The Enthusiast. It says I'm scatter-brained, spontaneous, and versatile. Also pretty damn accurate. Sure, there are things in these write-ups that I don't agree with, but in general, I fit into these categories.

I find these kinds of tests interesting and helpful because reading the results in depth can help you to learn who you are. You can decide whether they're accurate or bullshit, but developing self-awareness is an incredible skill that will help you love yourself fully.

Another benefit of these tests is that they let you know the kinds of people you are ultimately compatible with (both for platonic and romantic purposes), and who you're likely to butt heads with. Now, this isn't really helpful unless you know what your friends' results are, too, but it's an interesting starting point. I find it's helpful to add your personality types to your online dating profiles, because not only can you get a good idea who you might be uber-compatible with, but it might strike up a conversation.

I would never suggest not pursuing a relationship with someone just because a website tells you your four letter codes don't match up well. There have been countless examples of people having fun, healthy relationships while defying the algorithms these tests created. I will say that I am currently in the best, healthiest relationship of my life and our Myers-Briggs and Enneagram Personality Types are both the most compatible option for either of us.

Take a minute to go online and take these two tests. Write down your results below! (Resources at bottom of page)

The Myers-Briggs personality type I'm most compatible with is...

....

The Enneagram personality type I'm most compatible with is...

....

- *Take the test at www.16personalities.com to determine your Myers-Briggs personality type.*
- *Take the test at www.EnneagramInstitute.com to determine your Enneagram personality type.*

"Patience is not the ability to wait, but the ability to keep a good attitude while waiting." – Joyce Meyer

DATING

Just like making friends in high school, it was also easier for romantic relationships to blossom during frequent hangouts at lunch and in classes. Until I was twenty-four, I hadn't had a relationship that didn't start by turning my best guy friend into a boyfriend. Even though I've been out of high school for a decade, I know many people who are newly single and just figured out dating in the adult world is an entirely different beast. You have so much on the line!

Dating is adventure and a demon wrapped in one package. It's complicated, frustrating, and stressful, but it can lead to wonderful things. Unfortunately, the cliché of needing to kiss a lot of frogs before you find your prince(ss) is usually true. I've been in the world of dating myself many times, and I've watched my friends go through it in every imaginable way—in high school, after a divorce, long-distance, casually, and a whirlwind that ends up in an engagement after a few weeks.

Going on dates is scary, and you're truly putting yourself out there every single time you agree to meet someone new. You might feel an immediate connection, or you might throw up in your mouth when they try to kiss you. You could find it difficult to fit all the conversation you want into one evening or you could have an awkward-off with empty silences. It can be a real shit show, and I commend you for trying each and every time you do. First dates represent hope and optimism. They show that you're willing to try again. That is remarkable since you've (probably) had your heart broken before.

Not only is the internet great for meeting people with interests similar to you, but it's become the most common place for people to meet and start romantic relationships! I think it's silly for people to be embarrassed about using online dating websites to find a significant other. It's just another resource at our disposal. It helps you weed people out in advance! I've dated at least a dozen people I met off dating websites, and I never would have met any of them by conventional means. There is no wrong way to do things, and you should never feel shame or guilt for trying to go after something you want.

ONLINE DATING ADVICE

- Don't fill in any sections you don't want to. I actually recommend leaving things like "income" blank on purpose, as well as religion, unless it is a huge part of your life that could potentially be a deal breaker.

- Have at least three photos of yourself, including one full body shot.

- List things in your "Favorites" section, especially things that demonstrate your sense of humor (like your favorite TV shows, comedians, etc.).

- Give a call to action at the bottom of your profile. Remember these things are really awkward, so if someone wants to message you, but doesn't know where to start, give them an out! I wrote things like tell me who your favorite character is on Arrested Development, the corniest pick-up line you've ever heard, send me a photo of you shoving a cupcake into your mouth.

- Be prepared for creepy and disgusting messages. Block them, and move on.

- Answer as many of those personal "extra" questions as you can that let people know more about you and can bring up your initial "compatibility" percentage. These aren't all-telling, but it's a good starting point. It also lets people know you're serious about using the site.

- Message people first! People love getting messages on these sites because it means that someone was interested enough to put themselves out there. They might never see you if you don't say hi, so go for it! What's the worst that could happen?

- When you message people, say something interesting. "Hey, what's up?" is boring as hell. Answer any calls to action they have in their profile. Say something witty, or note a common interest.

- Give people chances. Some people don't photograph well, some are awkward online. If you think you might connect with them, go out for lunch and see what happens! It doesn't need to be love at first sight Just try.

As far as going on actual dates, love yourself to protect yourself. Tell a friend where you're going and as much info as you have about the person (their name, what kind of car they have). Meet in daylight in a public place and drive separately. Know the area you're going to, and if you keep mace in your purse, make sure you bring it. This isn't pessimism, this is preparedness.

Be on time, be kind, give genuine compliments. Demonstrate that you're strong, independent, and fabulous on your own. Offer to pay for what you ordered, and if they insist on paying you can let them, but remember that you never owe anyone anything. If you have ground rules, stick to them. If you don't want to kiss someone on the first date or sleep with them till after four dates, that's up to you! Remember you are in control. It's also probably not a good sign if someone isn't willing to compromise with you from the get-go. You also have the chance to relinquish consent whenever you want to. That said, there is nothing wrong with sleeping with someone when you first meet them if that's what you want. Priorities shift all the time, and sometimes you're trying to find the person you'll marry and sometimes you just want to get laid. Be safe, be conscious, make your own decisions. There is no judgment here.

"Don't settle for a relationship that won't let you be yourself."
– Oprah Winfrey

ROMANTIC RELATIONSHIPS

The only way to have an amazing romantic relationship is to love yourself first, with an overwhelming infatuation. You have to be smitten with yourself before you can fall head over heels for someone else in a healthy, good, lasting way. If you don't love yourself, you will accept the love you think you deserve, which probably won't be what you really deserve. (Remember my experience with the sleaze ball who was cheating on his girlfriend with me?) If you don't love yourself you won't know what your needs are, and you'll put yourself second always. If you don't love yourself, you'll be more likely to become codependent.

There are all types of romantic relationships; monogamous, open, polyamorous. There are hook-ups, casual dating, and engagements. What's important is you know what you want and don't settle for less. If you're not comfortable with having sex before you have feelings for someone, wait. If you know you can't commit to a monogamous relationship don't tell someone otherwise. Lay out what you want in your mind and to other people.

This also goes for deal-breakers! Is religion, political affiliation, or the desire to have kids in the future something that would make or break your decision to be with someone? Be upfront about what you want and need. You owe it to yourself to be happy and compromise as little as possible.

Whatever type of relationship you desire, your goal with a significant other should be to find someone who doesn't need you. You want to find someone who is actually just fine without you, but chooses to be with you because they love you and find you fucking fascinating (because you are).

Your partner should never try to change you or stifle your enthusiasm or passion. One of my least favorite things was when an ex would tell me to "please calm down" when I got excited about something. There's no reason to do that. You are a beautiful creature, and just because someone else isn't excited about the same things as you doesn't mean they need to prevent you from experiencing joy.

Even the most compatible couples have their issues, though. You should fight and argue sometimes. That's a reminder that you're two separate people and are still passionate enough to care about fighting. You should worry if you don't even have the energy to argue about something important to you because it might mean that you've become hopeless and complacent.

My instinct has always been to say I'm "fine" when my significant other asks me what's wrong. I say I'm fine over and over, even though we both know I'm lying, and then eventually I explode in a fit of irrational anger. The relationship I'm in now is different than the others I've been in for many reasons. I think one of the best things about us is I have made an effort to actually say what's bothering me when it's bothering me. I've also asked him to make sure, if I revert to old tendencies, to push and pull it out of me. It works incredibly well.

When I say I'm okay and I'm not, I begin spiraling inside my own mind. I create terrible situations and reasons for things that are based on imaginary nonsense, not reality. I start getting mad about things that haven't even happened yet! It's ludicrous. If I explain why I'm upset, it can usually be resolved quickly and without much pain. I'd say 60-70% of the time I'm upset about something, it's a misunderstanding. If I just say how I'm interpreting things, he can usually say "Oh, that's not what I meant!" or "Here's why..." and I feel better instantly. The other 30% of the time it's a real issue that needs to be addressed, so if I didn't bring it up that would be a disservice to both of us.

"Don't go to bed angry" is a good rule of thumb, but I don't think you need to wait all day. Stewing in your frustration isn't doing anyone good, and it can prevent you from completing tasks, being creative, or generally having a good time. Address what you can as soon as possible.

Besides dealing with issues as they arise, and being totally honest with your partner, I suggest you make time for three more things: sex, outings, and alone time. The main difference between the relationship you have with your best friend and a significant other is sex, let's face it. I tell my best friend the same things I tell my boyfriend, and we can do lots of the same activities. But I don't sleep with my best friend, nor am I attracted to her sexually. Sometimes it feels weird to think about sex being the only difference, but it's true when it comes down to it. That being said, make time for sex. I don't mean to schedule it, because spontaneity is important, but if you're both really busy all the time, it's easy for sex to get pushed to the side. Not only is sex a great stress reliever and way to practice self care, but it can really reconnect you with your partner. I also recommend cuddling naked before, after, or independently of sex. Just be with your person in an intimate way, talking, napping, laughing. It's important.

Make time to go out and do things, too. Going out to dinner is a good start, especially if you always eat at home, but try to plan activities that don't center around food! Dinner can be a cop out and something you do on auto pilot, so try to plan an activity. Think about where your interests overlap and schedule something you go out and do together.

UNCUSTOMARY DATE IDEAS

- Put on formal wear and go bowling
- Sing karaoke all cheesy or strange, or go to one of those places where you can film a video of you doing it
- Go on simultaneous scavenger hunts (you each make one for the other)
- Pretend you've never met and take on different personas
- Have a candlelit dinner at a fast food restaurant
- Take a road trip to something mediocre like a Sheetz that's forty-five minutes away
- Play hide and seek in a park
- Crash a wedding
- Come up with a make-out (or sex) bucket list and spend all night trying to check off as many places as you can
- Dress up as superheroes and walk old people across the street or stop petty crimes like jaywalking
- Plan out choreography and break it out at a bar or club
- Make the ultimate fast food feast, where you go to as many drive-thrus getting different items at each place
- Have a thrift store competition to see who can come up with the weirdest outfit in the dressing room
- Purchase a ride on a carriage and hang a sign (and cans) on the back of it that says "Just Dating" or "Still Married" while a horse walks you around
- Put a movie on mute and pretend you're the characters on *Mystery Science Theater 3000*
- Go to a Monster Truck Rally
- Paint each other
- Do some street performing – spray paint yourselves and become a statue or rap on the corner
- Recreate the orgasm scene in "When Harry Met Sally" when you go out to dinner
- Wear onesies that turn you into unicorns, dinosaurs, etc. and go on a "normal" date

Additional Date Ideas:

1.
....

2.
....

3.
....

As much as you need to make time for each other, you also need to spend time separately. Just going to work during the day in different buildings isn't enough, either. You need to make sure you're having a little bit of time allotted for you. Take yourself on dates like we talked about, or go out with your friends. Even the most compatible couples have interests that don't overlap. Make time to nurture those interests without your partner. Remember, you need to be an independent person who wants to be with your partner. Just because you're in a relationship doesn't mean you need to do everything together. The time apart from each other will make you miss and appreciate each other a little more. It adds intrigue and gives you more stuff to talk about. If you spend all day together, you'll have less conversation topics for dinner than if you had spent the day apart. Everything in moderation, babe.

"We assume that others show their love in the same way that we do and if they don't follow that equation, we worry that the love is not there." - Amy Przeworski

HOW WE SHOW LOVE

There are many different ways we show love, and most people gravitate towards one type of demonstration than others. The main "Love Languages" are words of affirmation, acts of service, gift giving, quality time, and physical touch. For example, I'm a huge gift giver, and enjoy showing how much I love someone with words. Those are my two main ways of showing love. My boyfriend's ways are quality time and physical touch, but that doesn't mean things don't work!

It's important to understand the Love Languages because it gets you more in touch with how you like to show and receive love, and can make your relationships (both platonic and romantic) stronger.

My best friend and boyfriend aren't big on gift giving at all. They love when I give them things because they know it comes from a place of love and demonstrates how much I care about them, but that's not how they choose to express love. They know to accept gifts I give them with enthusiasm and make a big deal about my birthday. I know not to get offended if they don't get as excited about something I got them, or if they don't remember to get me a gift for a special occasion.

There are a couple of easy online quizzes that you can take to determine what your main love language(s) are, but you can also just pay attention to what you and your loved ones respond to. Relationships are a two-way street, fueled on give and take. Making an effort to show love in a way that isn't as natural to you and making it known how you want love shown to you, is a way to practice self love. You have to teach people how to treat and love you. Making your needs known is a radical act.

What are your top two love languages?

1.

....

2.

....

"Surround yourself with the right people, and realize your own worth. Honestly, there are enough bad people out there in the world - you don't need to be your own worst enemy."
– Lucy Hale

DON'T WASTE YOUR TIME

So far, I've talked about making more friends, networking, and strengthening your new and existing relationships. What I haven't mentioned is not wasting your time on people who do nothing for you.

You don't need to be friends with everyone, and deciding that doesn't make you evil. I remember when the federal law for marriage equality was passed, I changed my profile picture to a rainbow version of myself and wrote a caption in celebration of the long overdue occasion. At the bottom of the caption I wrote, "And if you don't agree with my decision that's what the unfriend button is for". I got a lot of flack for that sentence, but I stand by it.

Marriage equality is something I'm very passionate about and I believe that your stance on the issue says a lot about who you are. I'm passionate about street art, glitter, and cat cuddles too, but I would never unfriend someone over their disinterest in those things. The concept of marriage equality is very simple to me, and I think if you truly believe two consenting adults of any gender, race, or culture shouldn't be able to get married, you're against human equality.

I am not Christian, a Republican, or supportive of gun-ownership, but I am not angry at Christians, Republicans, or gun-owners. I am friends with these people in real life and online, and our political differences don't mean we can't have a healthy, fun relationship.

I'm not gay and I will never marry a woman, but I will fight till I'm blue in the face for anyone's right to do so. My invitation to people who disagreed with the Supreme Court's decision to approve marriage equality in all fifty states was not one written out of hate. I do not hate them for their beliefs, but their beliefs make me feel that they hate the gay and transgender population, and that makes me want to not associate with them.

Me not wanting to be friends with someone doesn't mean I hate them. Surrounding yourself with people who inspire you and who aren't full of negativity will make your life happier and healthier. Self love is about surrounding yourself with positivity, and that includes people. Since I can't comprehend the idea of not agreeing with two adults' decision to marry each other regardless of their gender or sexual orientation, I choose not to associate with people who feel that way. That's all it is.

The above example is an issue that's divided my country, as well as others, and has been the reason for homicide, suicide, and terrorism. It doesn't need to be this severe. You can choose not to be friends with someone just because you don't like them or they don't make you feel good when you're around them.

Your time is precious, and wasting nights with people who do things you don't approve of, make you uncomfortable, pressure you into doing things, offend you, or you find boring isn't worth it! You have big things to do, babe. Stop wasting time on people who don't enhance your life.

Remember we need to take responsibility for our own happiness and I feel that this applies to people, too. There are a few people in my life that I have continued to hang out with despite their lack of courtesy or their obnoxious behavior. Time after time I end up going home frustrated, sad, or exhausted. I've realized that these nights are my fault.

Sure, the reason I'm so upset is because the person I was meeting was incredibly late, didn't plan, inconvenienced and took advantage of me, but history has proven that was going to happen. I knew full well it was a likely outcome and I still went, so that's what happened. I take responsibility for how I feel those nights because I know I can't control what other people do, I can only control my reactions to them. My reactions (and yours) include deciding whether or not you're even going to bother spending time with them in the first place.

"My family would be supportive if I said I wanted to be a Martian, wear only banana skins, make love to ashtrays, and eat tree bark." – Casey Affleck

SUPPORT SYSTEM

The point of all this is to connect with other like-minded people who are positive influences in your life and can provide you with a much needed support system. No matter how strong you are, you always need people in your life to help you. Nothing is ever accomplished alone.

I don't mean to insinuate that you aren't independent and capable, because you are, but even if you're not actually partnering with someone or asking for assistance, your achievements can probably be attributed to at least one other person in your life. That person might have been a teacher in elementary school who was the first person to tell you that you could rise above adversity to reach your dreams. It might be an aunt who let you move out of a terrible living situation, which allowed you to feel safe and grow as an individual.

Your support system can be any size and include anyone. They can be older, younger, local, across an ocean, a teacher, your psychiatrist, a family member, whoever. My hope is you will use the internet and networking to make new friends and do your best to create healthy, fun, and beneficial relationships. Work at your relationships. Put effort in to give as much as you get. A support system will help you achieve your career goals, go on adventures, and remind you you're amazing, beautiful, and weird when you're sliding into self doubt. A good support system is worth its weight in gold, and you deserve to have a great one.

In the next chapter we'll let our freak flag fly by using our unique qualities to succeed and soar.

THINGS TO TRY:

- Have a sleepover
- Talk on the phone with your friend, or leave a silly voicemail if they don't answer
- Take a class in something you're interested in
- Hold a meeting in an office supply store
- Play True American
- Make up a secret handshake
- Dance with strangers in public places
- Wear a name tag
- Have business cards printed
- Write thank you notes to someone new you met
- Take personality tests
- Take the Love Language test
- Make a list of ways someone can show you they love you
- Make a list of deal breakers for romantic relationship
- Go out of your way to show love to someone in a love language you don't identify with
- Join an internet group for one of your interests
- Ask a new friend how you can support them
- Say how you really feel when your significant other asks you how you are
- Generally rule out the term "I'm fine" from your vocabulary
- Make an online dating profile
- Sever ties with a toxic person in your life
- "Unfriend" toxic acquaintances on social media
- Observe the people around you; it might make for good conversation later
- Go on an uncustomary date
- Make your own list of uncustomary date ideas
- Research places you can meet people in your area
- Send party invitations in the mail

- Follow "similar" accounts on Twitter
- Make a list of your friends'/contacts' birthdays and send cards in the mail
- Work on your "elevator pitch" for meeting new peers
- Be positive
- Reach out to someone you've lost touch with and miss
- Friend people on social media after meeting them, and send them a personal message saying what a pleasure it was
- Create a tangible ice breaker (like business card packets)
- Follow through with plans, don't cancel last minute, and be on time
- Say yes to invitations people send you
- Use body language to show you're listening to others
- Be yourself when meeting new people, so new friends know the "real you"
- Think of conversation topics that fall somewhere between the shallow end of "the weather" and deep end of "abortion laws" so you're not boring or aggressive during conversation
- Have good manners
- Set a goal when you go to a social event to try to meet X number of people and get their contact info, even if that sounds silly
- Smile
- Don't worry if someone doesn't want to hang out with you or show interest in talking to you; not everyone is going to connect
- Forgive your friends for indiscretions the same way you'd want them to forgive you
- Put your phone away when you're with other people
- Be honest, but not mean
- Host and attend events where drinking isn't the main activity
- Make eye contact
- Ask people for their advice
- Ask people about themselves
- Make jokes

7

EMBRACING YOUR WEIRD

A huge part of self love is finding out what makes you unique and celebrating it with vigor. The first parts of our lives are full of pressure to fit in, but as you get older. you realize being original, unique, and downright strange is actually a good thing. Being a cookie cutter copy won't get you recognized from the rest of the crowd. Great success is usually bestowed on those who figure out they have something new to offer the world. The world usually responds with enthusiasm because they didn't even know they needed that thing!

This chapter will encourage you to and support all the things that make you strange including lifestyle choices and magic making.

IT'S OKAY TO NOT BE WHERE YOU THOUGHT YOU'D BE

When you're a teenager, you talk with your friends and write in your journal about what you want to do after you graduate high school. You think about when you'd want to get married and have kids, what your dream job would be, and what you'd want to study in college. Most of my friends made specific timelines for these milestones, which was great practice for goal-making and manifesting dreams. But you have to remember that those were dreams you made as an adolescent.

Think about all the things you've learned since you were a teenager. It's very important to have goals, but that doesn't mean you need to write things in stone and not allow any wiggle room or amendments along the way. When I was fifteen, I decided that I would graduate college when I was twenty-one, go on to get my Master's degree, be married by twenty-four, and have three kids by the time I was thirty. All of those things either didn't happen, or I no longer desire them.

Getting my Bachelor's in the minimum of four years became impossible, especially because I had a full-time job in the field I thought I wanted to work in while I was still in school. I worked thirty to forty hours a week and took at least twelve credits each semester to stay on my dad's health insurance. I worked my ass off, but that didn't mean I was "on schedule". By the time I graduated, my career goals had totally changed, and I had no interest in continuing an official education in graduate school.

By the time I was twenty-two, I realized the idea of being married in two years sounded ridiculous. I was still so young, and even though I was in a serious relationship, I had no intent to get married in the coming years. I also realized that I had no desire to actually have children. When I made that timeline in high school, I included kids because I thought I was supposed to. Everyone else planned on having kids, and I just figured I should as well. I started realizing that every interaction I had with small children made me uncomfortable, and I couldn't imagine raising my own.

Almost all of my close friends didn't follow the framework they created as an adolescent, either. I don't think that demonstrates a lack of achievement or follow-through. I think it's incredibly healthy. Adjusting to life as it comes and realizing your priorities can (and should!) shift is a part of being human. If I started having babies just because of something I wrote on a timeline twelve years ago, that would be stupid and irresponsible. Would you take advice from your fifteen-year-old-self on relationships or time management? Probably not, right? So why let your past self dictate your life's path?

It is one hundred percent totally okay to not be where you thought you would be as a kid. I think one of the reasons plans change is because we're all kids at heart. I know very few people who don't get frustrated with the requirements and responsibilities of being an adult. Having a set bedtime, making a budget, and dealing with conflicts at work aren't things we seek out and they're not really what we had in mind when we fantasized about adult life. Sure, we've experienced a ton of stuff since puberty and have gained a lot of wisdom, but we're always learning. At our core, we don't really know how to be adults. We're shown by example and draw information from all sorts of sources.

We still have to ask for help doing new things and procrastinate on deadlines as important as taxes. We still sometimes fashion our hair into a Mohawk when it's lathered up with shampoo, and think cookies taste better when they're in the shape of a dinosaur. If you were given the chance to jump in a ball pit, you might hesitate, but only for a second. The idea of playing might not be "grown-up" or "professional" but it's important for our mental health and inherent in our nature.

We're all just kids in adult costumes trying to figure out how to do everything in the best way. I still don't know the difference between baked and broiled, and get really whiny when I'm sick. We just move along, and do our best to make the most of each day. Sometimes those days teach us new skills that we can use in the future! Maybe next time you won't have to ask for help with something because you'll remember how to do it. Onlookers will say something like, "Wow, you've got it all figured out!" or "You're so put together!" and you'll laugh, just like every single one of us, and say to yourself, "Hahah. No, I really don't."

Even if you feel overwhelmed that you're not doing things the "right" way, I want you to know that you're really doing a great job. I'm proud of you. Don't compare yourself to your Facebook feed or people in your office. It's silly. There's plenty of stuff you know more about than they do, and we can all help each other out. Just do what feels right, babe. Your gut knows what you need. Practice self love, and embrace your life's journey, your decisions, and your progress.

Not being the "adultiest" adult isn't necessarily "weird", but it's important to remember that you should love yourself even if you haven't gotten to the point you thought you'd be at right now. If you had it all figured out, I think you'd be pretty fucking bored with this whole life thing.

"To be yourself in a world that is constantly trying to make you something else is the greatest accomplishment."
– Ralph Waldo Emerson

NON-CONFORMING CHOICES

In addition to not reaching milestones when you're "supposed" to, you actually don't ever need to reach a milestone if you don't want. This isn't the board game "Life", and you're totally allowed to skip over those mandatory squares where you buy a house, get married, and have kids. Nothing is required of you. If you decide not to do something the rest of your friends or family members have done, that does not mean you are incompetent or wrong. It means you're making your own path.

Not wanting kids is something I get a lot of flak for, but it doesn't change my feelings on the subject. I have a million reasons why I don't want to have kids, such as my lack of maternal instinct, not wanting to pass on my genetic material, and no desire to be tied down to another human for the rest of my life. It's not anyone's business, though, and neither are your choices or reasoning for them.

Often the reason someone might ask another person when they're having kids, or why they're not getting married is because they are ignorant to the concept of options and freewill against social norms. Sometimes they want to feel like other people are doing what they're doing. Sometimes they want to live vicariously through you. Sometimes they're just nosy. It doesn't matter. Remember you are never obligated to explain why you are or aren't doing something to anyone else. And also try not to interrogate others about their life choices, either. There are an infinite number of answers to the question you might ask, but the topic might touch a nerve.

Be steadfast in your choices. Stand firm and never apologize for them. If you don't want to go to your high school reunion because you have no interest in seeing people you could just stalk on Facebook if you so desired, RSVP "no". You never need to explain your decisions or your reasoning if you change your mind (because that's okay, too!). You are smart and strong.

Do what you want in a way that pleases you. It is okay to pay your bills on time but also charge two sumo suits to your credit card, to have a secure job with benefits and also have a ball pit in your basement, and to wake up early every day to go to the gym but make your alarm sound the theme song to "Duck Tales". Incorporate adult responsibility and childlike play as you see fit, without fretting over criticism or judgment.

YOU DON'T HAVE TOO MUCH TIME ON YOUR HANDS

Have you ever finished a project and had someone tell you, "You have way too much free time!"? They're wrong and ill-informed. You do not have too much free time, and this idea infuriates me.

"Free time" is a term we use to describe our lives when we are devoid of responsibilities. By responsibilities I mean things like work, school, and children. Time when we aren't expected to do anything specific, so we can do what we want. We can relax. We can work more. We can do whatever we want. It's our time. Therefore, the idea of having "too much" free time might just be indicating jealousy.

It is very true that some people don't have as many responsibilities as others. It's a giant spectrum. There are some people who don't have jobs or bills, and some people who are supporting the finances of more than just themselves. Some people have to take care of other living creatures from the time the alarm goes off till they crawl back under the covers, and some people sleep till noon and eat spaghetti all day in their pajamas. I recognize that discrepancy.

What bothers me is most of the time when Person A says that Person B has "too much free time" they are casting a judgment, i.e. that person has spent their time in a way the other never would have. Of course they did, though. Person A and B are completely different people. We all have different interests. Never tell a person that their interests are stupid.

This expression is something I've heard my whole life, and it's been said to me in an accusatory manner. When I was in high school, I used to make little goody bags full of candy and toys that I would pass out to my friends in the hallways. I would make these absurd greeting cards for my own fake company called "Sugar And Spice And Pubic Lice", congratulating the recipient on Not Dying Yet or Getting The Biggest Cheesesteak At Lunch. My friends, even the ones who were receiving the goody bags, would shake their heads while saying, "Wow, Mary. You have way too much free time."

At my old job, I started a custom called Wondrous Wednesdays, where I would make little treats for all of the employees in my building once a week. My boss let me know my coworkers were worried I was making these things during work hours (AKA stealing company time) since there's "no way" I would have done all that in my "free time".

I hear it when I do (elaborate) guerrilla art installations, and when I participate in a flash mob. How dare I go to multiple practices to prepare for a performance art piece that doesn't yield any monetary profit!? How dare I spend my time in a way that is different than you would!? Fuck that.

Most people think, since I don't have a corporate 9 to 5 job, I just have a ton of free time, and they're mostly right. I essentially turned my hobbies into my job, and I'm very lucky (and grateful) I was able to do so. But when I worked 35 hours a week, took four college classes a semester, and drove over a hundred miles every day, I still did the same stuff. If anything, I appreciated my free time more because of how little I had.

You can do whatever the fuck you want. Not just in your "free time", but in life. If you get home from work and want to veg out by binge-watching Netflix, then put on your fuzziest slippers, grab some delicious snacks and get to relaxing. If you want to pull a Leslie Knope, and when you get home from work you keep on working, then chug a Red Bull and color code some divider tabs with vigor. If you don't want to go to work at all and write the book of your generation instead, then pull up that roll-top desk, dip your feather in some ink... or just type on your laptop. Spend your free time doing things that make you happy. If other people don't get it, then don't invite them to your super cool success parties. And for the love of glitter, never be the person telling someone they have too much free time.

BEING STRANGE IN PUBLIC

Caring what other people think of you is a dangerous game. Doing or not doing something because you're worried about what a stranger or significant other might say is a slippery slope, because then you start living your life for others.

Selecting your wardrobe, music choices, or social activities because you want to appear a certain way is no way to live. Think about your fear, where does it stem from? What is the worst thing that happens if it's realized? A person you've never met before (and most likely will never see again) forms a quick judgment about you? So what?! They're gone, and you're out doing exactly what you want. It can become trickier when you're talking about your loved ones, but ultimately if someone you care about (and claims to care about you) can't accept you as you are, they might not be who you should be spending time with anyway.

I've found a really good way to kick start your self-esteem is to do something weird in public. It was a little weird walking along the street in booty shorts, a bright pink Troll wig, and a tank top that made me look naked from far away. After a few minutes I leaned into the role and became part of the story that those strangers would tell to their friends later that day or for years to come. I've had hilarious, amazing, strange experiences dressing up as a gypsy and walking around offering strangers a free reading of their future from a giant origami fortune teller. I've handed out lemons to people leaving a mall while wearing a shirt that has "LIFE" written on the front. Doing something bizarre in front of people I don't know is a huge confidence booster, because you are saying, "I don't care what you think. This is what I'm doing!" (It's also a big adrenaline rush, if you're into that.)

Being yourself is the truest form of self love. Ask yourself what you want to do, and then do it. It takes practice to not care what people think about you, but I promise life is better when you don't.

WAYS TO BE WEIRD IN PUBLIC

- Say, "I'm sure you're wondering why I gathered you all here," when people enter an elevator
- Go into a store with a sign that says "World's Best ____" and say "Congratulations!"
- Ask the pet store clerk how long the bird seed will take to turn into birds
- When someone knocks on your door, knock back – Take phone calls on a banana
- Put "try me" stickers on food items in the grocery store
- Sit next to someone on the phone and answer the questions they ask the person they're talking to while holding a phone to your head, if they ask you what you're doing just say 'Sorry, I'm on the phone"
- Run into a store and ask what year it is, after they respond scream "It worked!" and run back out
- Yell the theme from *Frozen* as you dump fruit into a public toilet
- High five strangers
- Pretend you're famous
- Pose as a mannequin in a window
- Ask store clerks for things that don't exist
- Sit down next to someone at Starbucks and start telling them your life story, beginning with your birth
- Have a sack race with display pillow cases in a department store
- Have a race with the motorized cart scooters
- Organize a flash mob
- Scream "I won" when you get money out of an ATM
- Freeze in motion
- Download the same playlist to your friends' iPods and press play at the same time, dance down the street

MAGIC

My whole life, I've noticed I have the ability to do weird things. For years I ignored them. Once I figured out they were strange, I pushed them down and pretended they didn't exist. For example, having premonitions such as dreams that come true the next day, or immediately knowing I'm about to run into a person. I could predict things dealing with colors and numbers. I could see words as I said them, visually typed out in front of my field of vision. When I heard certain words, I'd see an image or feel touch on my arm.

Some of the things I'm describing are a condition called Synesthesia, where some of the wires in my brain are crossed, making certain senses occur simultaneously. (There are lots of different types you can learn about; I have Grapheme-Color, Chromesthesia, and Auditory-Tactile.) I kind of figured the reason I felt like someone was stroking my arm when I heard an orchestra of violins and I could see auras around people's bodies was for the same reason, but that wasn't true.

Synesthesia might be difficult to understand if you haven't experienced it, but straight up magic? That's something most people don't believe I can do even if I explain it to them fully. You might be one of those people, and that's fine! I'm not offended, and it will in no way influence the way I live my life (and no one's opinion about your interests or lifestyle should influence yours). Regardless of whether you have actual abilities, you can still get on the magic train and be a witchy babe!

All things witchy scared me for most of my life. My mom was always interested in things like Tarot cards, crystals, and manifesting, and due to my complicated relationship with her (and the fact that being able to predict things freaked me out), I steered clear of all things related, even if I was innately drawn to them.

A very small percentage of my life has included learning more about aromatherapy, chakras, and the qualities certain gemstones possess. It's been really interesting and helpful to me, though, which is why I recommend it to you. Being in tune with the cosmos and holistic remedies can be extremely beneficial for your quality of life.

A simple place to start is by making an altar, just a designated space full of items that are important to you. Use it to prioritize your life and belongings, and sit in front of it to meditate (it's also a tangible reminder that you need to do it). Remember it doesn't need to be full of things you'd find in a store that reeks of sage, either.

My altar has crystals, candles, and incense on it but it also has things that are significant to me personally like confetti I collected from the floor of a Ke$ha concert, meaningful postcards sent to me in the mail, and a squishy felt heart. The lighter I use to light my candles has a logo from Broad City on it, because I find the stars of that show to be powerful feminists. Make it your own. You can add and take things off your altar as frequently as you want, and it can be as large or small as you decide or can accommodate. Mine is on the bottom shelf of a cabinet that also houses DVD's and my necklace stand.

IDEAS FOR THINGS TO PUT ON YOUR ALTAR IF YOU DON'T KNOW WHERE TO START:

- Crystals
- Stones
- Incense
- Candles
- Dried, pressed, or fresh flowers
- Visualization board
- Quotes
- Meaningful pictures, notes, mementos, mail
- Confetti
- Fabric
- Scarves
- Petals
- Sage
- Trinkets
- Totems
- Jewelry
- Written affirmations
- Seashells
- Keys
- Tarot cards
- Religious symbols
- Containers of sand or dirt from trips
- Prayer cards
- Boxes
- Magic wands
- Leaves, branches
- Worry stones
- Beads

NOT LETTING OTHER PEOPLE AFFECT YOU

Sure, you should never alter your lifestyle to make someone like you or make them feel more comfortable, but that's easier said than done. We're faced with pressures from all over the place to fall in line, conform, or do things differently.

When you're dating, it's tempting to tell white lies so the person you're seeing wants to see you again. You might apologize for still living at home with your parents. You might pretend you're way more into Queen than you are (but seriously, why don't you like Queen?). Or you might say you've slept with less people than you have. None of that is necessary, darling. You are who you are. If this date is going to turn into a meaningful relationship, it should begin with honesty.

Sometimes it's easier to lie when you go home to visit your parents, at a bar with a new group of friends, or in the doctor's office. We always want to shine the most flattering light on ourselves. Admitting you aren't getting that promotion, aren't into clubs anymore, or haven't flossed in six years can feel embarrassing.

Your life isn't embarrassing, though. Even if someone does something differently or "better" than you, I can name a dozen things right off the bat that you can do "better" than them! People are always in different phases of their life's journey and they learn at different rates on different subjects. I, like many people, value honesty. Telling people what's really going on is more likely to make them respect you more than that white lie you were about to tell them.

This isn't to say that you should go out of your way to hurt someone's feelings. You're the best judge of your life, and if you think it will devastate your mom when you confess that you hated her pot roast, then just smile and make yummy noises. Use your discretion when telling the (whole) truth. My point is, you never need to apologize for your life or choices. Some people aren't going to like you or what you do, and no amount of explaining or debating is going to change that. Accepting that you won't please everyone is one giant step for self love, bigger than that one Neil Armstrong took. It makes everything easier.

When you accept you're going to piss people off, you start living. Have you ever changed your outfit before leaving the house, not because it was uncomfortable, but because you were worried someone wouldn't think you looked attractive in it? Have you ever agreed to go to an event, not because you wanted to go, but because you didn't want to upset a friend? Imagine wearing what you want, saying what you want, and going the places you want to go without worrying if you'll ruffle feathers. Be respectful and considerate as a human being, but beyond that, you should feel free to do what you desire.

BURNS

Have you heard of Burning Man? Probably. Do you know more than "it's a festival in the desert"? That's okay, I didn't really know much about it either. When I started dating my boyfriend, Joe, he welcomed me into his friend group full of "burners". These people are extremely awesome, nonjudgmental, and wonderfully strange so when I found out they all went to this thing called "Playa" and collectively adored the experience enough to go fifteen different times, I had to know more about it.

For months, all I knew was I was "going to love it". I asked lots of questions, especially ones about what I needed to bring for camping because I had never been camping (except once when I was seven in the Girl Scouts, but we slept in bunk beds in a cabin, so I'm pretty sure that's not camping). Everyone told me burns were hard to explain and I didn't understand how true that was till I went to one myself.

The first burn I went to was called Playa Del Fuego. Like many other regional burns, it's sponsored by Burning Man and has the same set of principles as the main event in the desert of Nevada. There are ten principles including inclusion, self reliance, self expression, gifting, civic responsibility, and participation.

Burns are at least a few days long and generally held in a large open space. People bring their own camping equipment and set up in a way to sustain themselves for their entire stay; almost no one leaves the grounds once they're there. You don't pay for anything once you're in, either. If someone asks you for something and you can reasonably accommodate them, you do. If you need something, you ask for it and it will easily be provided to you. There will be a main event at least one of the nights where a large wooden sculpture, made specifically for this occasion, will be lit on fire. Everyone will stand around it, watching the process of its burn, then dance around the ashes.

You might think everyone at a burn would be a stereotypical hippy in flowing skirts, rattling a tambourine around with their eyes closed, and you're wrong. I mean, those people exist and they come to burns, but it's just as diverse as my high school's lunchroom. All types of people come, and you are always welcome. The overwhelming atmosphere of nonjudgmental welcoming will make you wish you didn't have to go back home.

This is a place where your inner weirdness is celebrated to the fullest extent. There are bizarre and creative events, food, and clothing as far as the eye can see. At Spring Playa there is a naked slip 'n slide where no photographs are allowed. It's a completely safe space where everyone is one hundred percent in-the-moment. If you're on the sidelines, you get to witness naked bodies of all shapes and sizes running at full speed, launching themselves onto a giant wet plastic mat. If you're participating, you get the adrenaline rush of running naked in front of a supportive crowd and sliding fifty feet across a field. I think running naked might be the least "flattering" thing for anyone, but no one is hung up on body image. All you'll see are bare butts and smiles.

Between all the costumes, twinkle lights, and enormous balloon arch, I had never felt more at home anywhere. I knew immediately I would be back next time, even if the whole sleeping outside and having to make my own food (read: ask Joe to please make me food) still isn't my favorite thing in the whole world.

I'm telling you about this experience to let you know there is always more to discover. I went twenty-six years without realizing I could drive two hours to find heaven-on-earth. There are plenty of people out there who "get" you and would love to spend time with you in a way you both find fun. There is a place where what's considered weird at your office is considered natural to everyone else. This place might not be Playa, Burning Man, or whatever regional burn there is near you, but there is something out there that will make your heart soar. If what makes your heart soar has been considered strange by everyone in your life until now, that's okay. Hope is not lost. Your fellow weirdos are out there, waiting for you.

In the next chapter we will talk about one of the toughest and most important aspects of self love: accepting who we are.

THINGS TO TRY

- Write down all the ways you've made your teenager-self happy
- Do something from the "Ways To Be Weird In Public" list
- Add three of your own ideas to that list
- Create an altar
- Stand up for your choices
- Go to a regional burner event
- Have your aura photographed
- Take a mime class
- Go planking
- Make a list of all your unusual qualities and talents
- See a sideshow performance
- Explore abandoned buildings
- Get a Tarot card reading
- Learn to juggle
- Try to photobomb a stranger or appear in the background of a newscast
- Walk around a park with a pepper bottle saying, "Fresh ground pepper?"
- Turn your car into an art car
- Put up flyers that have a picture of your pet with the text "Not lost, just bragging"
- Refer to Cheerios as donut or bagel seeds
- Name your inanimate objects and electronic items
- Carry around a plastic pipe
- When people ask you to dress up, just add a top hat to whatever you're currently wearing
- Ignore people who tell you that you have "too much free time"
- Wear costumes and play dress up
- Speak in puns

8

SELF ACCEPTANCE

So far, I've talked about ways to make your life full of as much happiness and meaning as possible, which are direct ways to practice self love. As much as self love is a non-linear journey throughout your entire life, I do consider self acceptance to be something a little more advanced. Accepting who you are, and screaming it out loud to the world is a pretty powerful act. I want you to be able to do that with confidence and flair without second guessing yourself.

This chapter will cover one of the most difficult tasks in the journey of self love: accepting who you are to the core, including your physical body and personality.

"You yourself, as much as anybody in the entire universe, deserve your love and affection." – Buddha

SELF WORTH

Having a positive self-image is vital to practicing self love and being happy. You should believe that you are enough, that you are worth it, that you deserve the best. It's pretty hard to do, though.

It's likely that for most of your life you've felt obligated to demonstrate your worth to other people. We get judgment and criticism from our parents, peers, teachers, doctors, coworkers, friends, significant others, strangers, and so on. When we're constantly being judged, or at least feel like we are, we often find it necessary to prove that we're good enough.

Having self worth means valuing yourself and who you are as a person. It's about having an intrinsic belief that you matter.

We all have a little voice in our head that has told us, at some point, that we suck. That voice has told you your stomach is disgusting and your pores are huge and you shouldn't bother going out because there's no way that someone could ever love you. Some people's voice is louder than others and some voices arrive way earlier than others. You might make it all the way to high school before you hear your inner voice condemning your body and personality, but I think it's a safe bet to say that she's popped up more than once by now.

Building your self worth is about telling that voice to shut the hell up. You have to be firm and mean to it. Imagine you're on a debate team and your only goal is to counter the points this little voice is making. This voice is saying you don't deserve happiness. Why, voice? Fuck you. Of course I do. I deserve happiness the same way my best friend, mother, and neighbor do. I have value and I deserve to take up space!

Having a high sense of self worth and esteem can feel a bit narcissistic, but that's okay. It's a good, natural kind of narcissism. It's the kind you were meant to have. Your human right is to believe in yourself. If you have no ego you have no faith in yourself, and if you lack faith in yourself, you'll find it much harder to succeed.

Working on increasing your feelings of self worth will help you find it easier to love yourself, and loving yourself is the key to unlocking self acceptance.

STEP 1

Establish that you are worthy of existing on this planet.
You have just as much right to be here as anyone else, and
existing comes with the right to be happy.

STEP 2

Love yourself. Tell yourself you are amazing, beautiful, and
weird in all the best ways. Hug yourself with your thoughts
the way you would hug your best friend after they get home
from a six month trip.

STEP 3

Accept yourself as you are. Declare that you are here as-
is, and ready to conquer! If anyone doesn't like it, they can
promptly move on because you don't have any time to waste.
There's life to live.

"When nobody celebrates you, learn to celebrate yourself. When nobody compliments you, then compliment yourself. It's not up to other people to keep you encouraged. It's up to you. Encouragement should come from the inside."
– Joel Osteen

CELEBRATE YOUR STRENGTHS

Accepting yourself is about being satisfied with who you are. It's easier to be satisfied with yourself when you focus on your good qualities. Don't just be optimistic about life, be optimistic about yourself! What are your strengths in life? Think about your skills in the areas of interpersonal communication, creativity, kinesthetics, logical reasoning, mathematics, exploring, philosophy, writing, cooking, organizing, planning, sports, driving, fashion, photography, etc.

What are your strengths?

1.
....

2.
....

3.
....

4.
....

5.
....

Self deprecation isn't cool, and acknowledging what you're amazing at isn't narcissistic. You know that scene in "Mean Girls" where they're all standing in front of the mirror complaining about their bodies? They take turns scrutinizing their hair lines and nail beds before they look expectantly at Cady who hasn't offered up any body bashing of her own. In an attempt to fit in, she sheepishly offers up the fact that she has bad breath in the morning.

If you feel the need to put yourself down to be accepted in your friend group, you're surrounding yourself with the wrong people. Unfortunately it's not always pressure from something as small-scale as our social circles. Our society as a whole tells us it's better to never be content with how we look and who we are. That is bullshit, and if you've learned anything by now it should be that.

You are sexy. You deserve to take up space, be complimented, and feel beautiful. You should find it easy to list your good qualities. You shouldn't feel weird writing a resume or About Me page on your blog because you feel like it's weirdly "braggy". You're fucking awesome. Tell the world just how awesome you are.

"When I accept myself, I am freed from the burden of needing you to accept me." – Steve Maraboli

NOT COMPARING

When I was ten years old, in 1998, and my teacher asked us to write a paper on what we thought life would be like in 2010, we all agreed we'd be wearing space suits, driving hover cars, and living with a robot maid. Well, we're well past 2010 and it doesn't look like I'm getting my hover car any time soon, but what we do have is a ton of technology. It's pretty remarkable the way things have advanced. I've already talked about how perfect the internet can be for finding like-minded friends, but it comes at a price.

Social media is kind of a dragon you have to wrestle to the ground and if you win you get to ride around everywhere on a dragon. If you don't win you get eaten, or at least swallowed up by a million status updates that have the potential to make you feel inferior.

If I had a nickel for every time I heard a friend or coworker complain about how many people were getting engaged or having babies on their Facebook feed, I'd be able to buy a bunch of pretzel hot dogs at the Amish market. Why do we get so worked up about this stuff? Remember that it's okay to not be where you thought you'd be by now. So why do we care if other people are hitting milestones before us?

What's worrying me more lately is, in addition to people worrying that they won't get married by the time they're thirty, I'm hearing complaints that their lives are "boring". If I ask why they think that, they'll point to their phone, where there's a picture of someone they went to high school with parasailing over the ocean. So what?

Remember that if you feel a jealous twinge, it's a call to action. That means you need to go do something to get you closer to the goal you've created for yourself (or set that goal in the first place). However, getting yourself all worked up because someone is doing something fun on a Tuesday when you're scheduled to work is pretty ridiculous.

People post the good stuff online. Almost exclusively. They post pictures of their vacation, new baby, and engagement ring. They'll share when they get a promotion at work or are having a really good hair day. What percentage of your online friends are sharing pictures of screaming kids spilling grape juice on white rugs and smeared mascara after a fight with their spouse? Pretty small, right? Right.

I personally don't think there's anything wrong with only posting the good stuff if that's what you're into. The real world and news sites can be full of tragic events, so logging onto social media to see a brand new puppy or to find out someone paid for your friend's coffee in front of them at the drive-thru can be a breath of fresh air. I try to post as many colorful, upbeat, fun things on the internet as I can for this reason, but I also try to post reminders that real life is hard and no one is alone.

The first step in not comparing yourself to other people online is to realize that no one is giving a totally accurate depiction of their life, and you can be sure no one's situation is "perfect". The second step is to not care if you find out that's not true.

Remind yourself that we're all different, and just because someone else has something you don't (yet) doesn't mean you're any less powerful or wonderful. If you had a conversation with this person you're comparing yourself to, I'm positive they'd find something you do better than they do.

When we're doing all this comparing, we tend to compare the parts we feel are the weakest and worst about ourselves to the highest, most actualized qualities of others. How is that fair?! You're way too amazing to even begin to compare yourself to anyone anyway. You're complex, unique, and priceless. I'd have to make a really complicated diagram to effectively do all this comparing you're interested in doing, and "ain't nobody got time for that"!

Speaking of which, there are only 1,440 minutes in every day. If you're getting your eight hours of sleep, we're down to less than a thousand minutes left to get dressed, eat breakfast, and take on the world. Are you going to bother wasting those precious minutes on comparison? Not only is that not great time management, but nothing good ever comes of these comparison scenarios we drum up in our minds. What's the best scenario of spiraling for twenty minutes about how you wish you could have X, Y, and Z like Jenny or whoever? You'll just feel less happy and motivated to do all those amazing things you want to do.

Believe me when I say you're already cool. You're cool like Fonzie.

"As you build trust in yourself, your ability to expand your vision and fully live in your magnificence is amplified."
– Miranda J. Barrett

TRUST YOURSELF

Accepting who you are and embracing your uniqueness can feel unnatural because it's ultimately about taking a leap of faith in yourself. If you trust yourself, you'll find it easier to stick up for your choices, beliefs, body, etc. Your inner critic might make it feel like you can't trust yourself, but it's wrong. You're the only person who has been with you every step of the way so far, and you're the only one guaranteed to be there till the end. You have to have your own back. You have to feel so strongly about yourself that you'd stand on top of a mountain and declare your love for yourself in a scream that echoes down in the valley.

If your friend was in a toxic relationship where her boyfriend cheated on her, she might find it difficult to trust men in the future. Would you tell her to stop trying to find love because of that one guy? I hope not. A negative experience doesn't dictate your future, and it can't be used as a bargaining chip for pushing away potential happiness. You have to build up your trust after years of your inner critic shouting negativity and reasons for doubt at you the same way you would after a toxic relationship.

Accepting past negative experiences allows you to move on. Forgive your inner critic, trust your ability to make the right choices from now on, and begin living a life of color and beauty.

"When we're awake in our bodies and senses, the world comes alive. Wisdom, creativity, and love are discovered as we relax and awaken through our bodies." - Tara Brach

BODY LOVE

I want to re-emphasize the importance of loving your body. Loving your body can be very hard, especially at first. As much as I think that self love should be about loving who you are as a whole person, focusing on your personality, skills, potential, strengths, quirks, purpose, etc., I believe a lack of confidence in your physical body can end up trumping any intrinsic confidence you have. It actually makes sense to fall in love with your physical body first, so you can focus on loving the rest of you. And once you love the rest of you, it will be a lot easier to deflect any doubts that may pop up about your appearance in the future.

Going out in public in a bikini can be just as hard for someone who fits in a size two dress as it is for someone who wears a size twenty-two. That said, wearing a bikini at any size doesn't automatically indicate bravery. When Lena Dunham started showing her naked body in her show Girls, people told her she was brave. People tell Mindy Kaling it's great she has "so much confidence". The truth is, Lena loves her body, so she is comfortable being naked and it's not an act of bravery for her. Saying she's brave for taking off her clothes implies she has a reason to be ashamed of her body. Mindy doesn't understand why she wouldn't have confidence because she's so clearly awesome. Being surprised she has a high level of self confidence implies you think she doesn't deserve to feel that way.

Everyone deserves to feel comfortable in their body and confident in who they are. Your dress size and weight don't determine confidence, nor does the color of your eyes, hair, skin, or nipples. Be proud of your body if you are thin, muscular, soft, or fat. You have every right to love the physical vessel that transports your soul and dreams around this world if you have a thigh gap, feet so small you shop in the children's section of the shoe store, or hair so thick it turns into a forest at the first sign of humidity. There are benefits to every size and physical attribute. Find your own Sparkly Lining.

What is one part of your body you aren't crazy about or have struggled with disliking in the past?

....

How is that part of your body actually awesome in its current state? What's the silver lining of having it exist the way it is?

....

....

"In an extroverted society, the difference between an introvert and an extrovert is that an introvert is often unconsciously deemed guilty until proven innocent." – Criss Jami

INTROVERT VS. EXTROVERT

Myers-Briggs Personality Test tells me that I am an ENFP. There are two letter options for each category of the test, making there a total of eight letters. At some point in my life I've been each of those letters. I've been ENTJ, ESFP, ENFJ, etc. The only consistent thing throughout my life has been the E, which stands for Extroverted.

The main difference between extroverts and introverts is the way we gain our energy and obtain pleasure. Extroverts get their energy from being around other people and need a little more external stimuli to feel satisfied, whereas introverts need to "recharge" with ample alone time and don't need as many stimuli to arouse their pleasure centers.

There is no black and white system to defining an extrovert or introvert. It's a vast spectrum. As I get older I enjoy spending more time alone, but it's really just because I'm getting more comfortable with myself as I age, not because I'm becoming introverted.

I bring this up because I'm writing this book as an extrovert. I'm sure being extroverted is only one of many biases that has influenced my writing thus far. However, I want to let you know that if I've suggested anything that you don't feel comfortable doing, then you shouldn't do it. And if I've written from a point of view you've had more difficulty identifying with, I apologize.

There's definitely something to be said for magic happening outside of your comfort zone, but that's not the only place magic exists. Yes, I think trying things you haven't done before or that scare you a little bit can end up being largely beneficial. Stepping outside your comfort zone for an afternoon can open your eyes to things you didn't know you'd enjoy, but it can also make you have a panic attack!

Knowing who you are and what you like is important. We spend so much of life trying things out in these guess, test, and fail scenarios. If, after years of experimenting, you find something that brings you a lot of joy, hold onto it. It's okay to stop searching when you find your happy place.

If you enjoy spending most of your time alone at home, and have gone against your instincts for years to appease your friends with trips to bars and concerts, it's okay to finally say no to their invitations and stay in more. If your happy place is in your bedroom, make that space as special as you can and own your decision to do so.

Of course, if you expect to maintain relationships you need to put forth effort, and if you ever feel like you're getting in a rut, that's a call to action for change. But it's okay to be content. One of my favorite movie scenes is when Harriet the Spy is making her lunch for school at the kitchen counter. Her mother is suggesting all these other options because she's taken the same sandwich to school every day since she started. Harriet slaps some more mayonnaise on a slice of bread and says, "I can't help it if I know what I like, and I know what I like… tomato."

Also, the internet is full of extroverts. When you're scrolling through your newsfeed, you might feel pressured to go skydiving, have a YouTube channel, or take photos of you and your friends jumping on the beach in bikinis. You don't have to do any of that stuff. The reason it seems like there's more of that on your newsfeed is because we need attention, so we post our shenanigans all the time. Don't feel like you need to "do more" to be an interesting, worthwhile individual. Do more of what you love, not what other people love.

"If your compassion does not include yourself, it is incomplete." – Jack Kornfield

COMPASSION

By definition, in order to have compassion you have to recognize the suffering of someone or something. Being compassionate towards yourself isn't really any different from being compassionate for a good friend, a person you see on the street, or an animal. Having self compassion is acknowledging that you're experiencing some sort of pain and demonstrating concern and sympathy for that situation.

If you're feeling compassionate for someone, you are kind to them and provide sympathy instead of being mean, judgmental, and critical of their choices. If you see a homeless person panhandling on a street corner, you might feel sympathy for their lack of safety, nutrition, and a place to sleep instead of assuming they were kicked out of their homes for being abusive to their family or having a drug addiction. Compassion is also about knowing that someone has a drug addiction, and still feeling sympathetic to their current situation, regardless of their past history.

As we talked about in Self Care, you have to be nice to yourself the way you would be nice to your best friend. No one is perfect, and no one said you have to be. Looking past imperfections in your best friend or significant other is the same concept you should apply to yourself.

We all fuck up. A lot. Maybe in certain areas we fuck up less and less as time goes on, but sometimes we have giant relapses. Making mistakes is normal, expected, and part of growth. It's okay to regret something because it means you're learning, but it's not okay to let that regret interfere with growing after that experience. You're going to fuck up over and over because you're a (very beautiful) human being. It doesn't make sense to berate yourself each time you make a mistake! It hinders your personal progression, and remember that we never peak in development; we only constantly improve.

At the first burner event I attended, my camp was sitting down relaxing after setting up a dozen tents, giant shade structure, and kitchen equipment in the rain at dusk. We were pretty exhausted and my friend Phoenix said she thought we did alright setting up this year. I was one of four new people to the camp, and she looked at us and said, "We know we're probably never going to be good at this, but our goal is to suck a little less each year, and we did". Obviously the wording is meant to be a joke, but I thought that sentiment was beautiful. Maybe we'll never be perfect, even at something we're deeply passionate about, but that doesn't mean we can't keep getting better.

Give yourself a break. Actually, give yourself a literal break. Sometimes you need to just stop working and chill for a bit. Allowing yourself time to recuperate from a heavy workload or traumatic experience is a great act of self compassion. Would you tell someone else to take a break if they were doing what you're doing? Then give yourself permission to take one yourself.

What you don't want to do is pity yourself. It's always okay to feel sympathy and compassion for yourself, but pitying yourself and feeling like you're a disappointment is moving straight past self love into the territory of doubt and loathing. What you're going through right now may not be ideal, but remember the basics. You have to keep a positive attitude as best you can! There are always options and room for improvement.

You might even have traits you don't like. Maybe you respond with sarcastic comments when you're feeling defensive or act mean to fit in with new friend groups, but you wish you wouldn't. It's easy to develop defense mechanisms over time and it can be hard to get rid of them. Accept and forgive yourself when these traits pop up in conversation. Making a mistake or falling back into old habits doesn't make you a bad person!

Forgive yourself and give yourself permission to grieve when things don't work out, though. Grieving isn't exclusively reserved for death, it is necessary for any type of traumatic event, even figuring out that one of your childhood dreams isn't coming true. It's important to go through the grieving process when something bad happens in your life. Your grieving process might be a few hours, weeks, or years depending on what the situation is, but it's okay to give yourself time to grieve.

"Negative emotions like loneliness, envy, and guilt have an important role to play in a happy life; they're big, flashing signs that something needs to change." – Gretchen Rubin

EXPERIENCING EMOTIONS

Grief isn't the only emotional experience you need to let wash over you as necessary. We tend to think having emotions like anger, jealousy, fear, and sadness are negative and undesirable. It's part of the reason those aren't things we really share with our online friends or acquaintances. We keep things "light". We focus on things that make us happy, satisfied, excited, and hopeful. Joy is the ultimate goal, yes, and I'm a huge advocate for doing anything and everything that brings you happiness, but there is a hell of a lot more to the emotional spectrum.

If you haven't seen Inside Out, I recommend it. It was a great commentary for all ages on how we experience emotions. We prioritize happiness and attempt to ignore everything else. Sadness, anger, and fear all have their place. Without them we would be dull. Without them true happiness wouldn't be as incredible.

Lean into your emotions. When you're sad, wash off your mascara, draw the blinds, and remove any plans you had for getting out of your pajamas off your mental to do list. You can cry in the shower, wallow over a bar of chocolate, and zone out with Netflix while you feel melancholy.

When you're mad, throw (safe) things around, punch pillows, and scream as loud as you can. Listen to loud music and rearrange your room in a haphazard way. TYPE IN ALL CAPS, say "fuck" a lot, and go to the gym to run and lift weights.

It's all okay. I've kind of found if you throw yourself into your emotion with full force, you get sick of it quicker. Misery and fury can be weirdly satisfying, but it takes a ton of energy to stay that way! If you use up all your energy in a shorter, condensed period you're more likely to get fed up with it and move on.

What emotion are you the most afraid of?

....

What are three ways you can lean into that emotion next time you start feeling it?

1.
....

2.
....

3.
....

"To be yourself in a world that is constantly trying to make you something else is the greatest accomplishment."
– Ralph Waldo Emerson

ACCEPTING VS. RESIGNING

Just because you are accepting yourself as you are doesn't mean you are giving up on yourself or life. Can you love and accept yourself as an overweight person and still want to lose weight?

Yes. Can you love and accept yourself while you work your way up the ladder in your profession and still work your butt off for a promotion? Of course. Improvement is possible. Acceptance is necessary.

Self help and improvement is all around us. We always have the opportunity to utilize resources which will help us manage our time better, sculpt the muscles in our arms, and negotiate with coworkers. There are thousands of books to read, classes to take, and gurus to hire to help you work on all types of skills, but acceptance comes from within.

There is nothing wrong with working on improving parts of yourself. Where do we draw the line, though? Will there ever be a point where you rest and take a step back to appreciate all the progress you've already made? There needs to be times where you acknowledge the work you've been doing and celebrate who you are and how far you've come. If you put a check box in a goal on your Self Improvement To Do List and immediately set to work on the next item, you'll never have time to appreciate who you are.

Self love is understanding you're struggling with your mental health, but recognizing you're important enough to make it a priority to get help. It's adoring your body as it is, but deciding to start incorporating exercise into your lifestyle to make your stay on this earth a little longer.

Really, self acceptance comes when you're already taking care of yourself, practicing gratitude, staying positive, and embracing your unique qualities. This is an advanced stage of self love which doesn't come easy. You deserve to feel completely comfortable with yourself. Work until you can truly believe the words coming out of your mouth when you say, "I am who I am and I don't care whether you like it or not". In the last chapter we we'll explore our extensive opportunities for a fun, successful, love-filled life.

In the last chapter we we'll explore our extensive opportunities for a fun, successful, love-filled life.

THINGS TO TRY:

- Write down things you're good at
- Print your own "I Am Awesome" certificate
- Keep a document of all the compliments and nice things people say to you to remind yourself why you're great as you are
- Wear a bikini to the beach, regardless of your body size
- Make a list of things you've accomplished this year, or throughout your life
- Take selfies, because your face is pretty enough for the internet
- Stop apologizing for having opinions or taking up space
- Fill in this mantra: "I am already wonderful because:____ "
- Allow yourself to experience all emotions naturally, even the "negative ones"
- Stop scrolling through your social media feeds if you find that you are comparing yourself to your online friends
- Make note of times you start judging your body in the mirror or comparing it to someone else's, then actively think of three beautiful parts of your body
- List your imperfections and why you're grateful for them
- Write a mini biography, just a page or two long, that brags about all your accomplishments so far and who you are in general
- Write a nice note to yourself on your bathroom mirror (either with your finger so it shows up after you shower, or with dry erase markers
- Adopt the theory that correction is great, but condemnation is not
- Allow yourself to have bad days without thinking they are steps backward
- Remove the phrases "I suck" and "I hate myself" from your vocabulary
- Practice positive self talk
- Tell your inner critic to shut the hell up

- Think about who you would be as the highest potential/best version of yourself and list ways you are already on the road to being that person
- Make a list of things you are proud of
- Make a self portrait with any medium, demonstrating how sexy you are
- Accept compliments with grace, but know you damn well deserve them
- Make a personal manifesto
- Stand naked sans make-up in front of a mirror and say "I accept my imperfections and love myself"
- Make eye contact with yourself in the mirror
- Understand you can't make everyone happy; so as long as you are happy with yourself everything is going great
- Any time you have a thought of self doubt, say "NOPE! I am awesome" instead
- Make a kissy face to yourself in the mirror
- Realize what triggers you have about self doubt or when you do things you might not want to do

9
DREAMS & GOALS

We've talked about a lot so far. My goal, intent, and hope is for you to build yourself up from the ground level. To find out who you are and love that person unconditionally, create an environment in your house and mind for growth, and then take on the world. The point of loving yourself is to be happy, and to be truly happy we need to keep moving forward, creating goals, and chasing dreams.

In this final chapter we'll talk about setting goals, manifesting their outcome, and celebrating your successes

"Keep your dreams alive. Understand to achieve anything requires faith and belief in yourself, vision, hard work, determination, and dedication. Remember all things are possible for those who believe." – Gail Devers

DREAMING

You are important. You are extremely important. Your thoughts, actions, body, and dreams are all important and need to be nourished with encouragement. Your biggest desires in life deserve to be heard, and more importantly, reached with flourish! There's no reason you can't be the artist in the museum you walk around in, the author in the bookstore you frequent, or the architect of the church you attend. Those people all exist and they might as well be you! You have to believe, you have to want it, and you have to get busy working!

Reaching your goals can be a long and difficult journey, but it's not impossible.

What would you try to do if you knew you could not fail? Your answers to that question are dreams! Think about your wildest, most outrageous fantasies and write them down. No one's looking. This is just for you.

1.
....

2.
....

3.
....

4.
....

5.
....

Making your dreams come true is simpler than a flick of your sparkly magic wand. though. There are a ton of small and big steps to take on your way to actualization, but every single step you take is success! Achieving a small goal is just as important as the end goal, because it's setting the foundation you require for not sinking into the mud.

It sounds trite, but life is fucking short. Think about ten years ago. Where were you? What were you wearing? Who were you spending your time with? What were you doing? Who were you? Does it seem like it was really ten years ago? Probably not. It might not seem "like yesterday", but it probably doesn't feel like an entire decade has passed.

An enormous amount of change can happen in one year, let alone ten. Look at fashion as an easy example! From the 50s to the 90s we went from poodle skirts to "Go-Go" boots to bell bottoms to blown out bangs to heroin chic. The transformation was gradual, but as time passed enough changes were made that we can have totally different chapters in textbooks dedicated to each ten year period of fashion!

If you're lucky, you'll live about eighty years. The first twenty five percent of that life is spent as a child, in school, lacking an "adult" status. Then you have forty years to figure out who you are, develop a style, and find your purpose. About four decades to find a job that makes you money so you can throw a party to celebrate your relationship with a life partner, travel the world to experience different cultures, and find a place to live that feels like home. You don't have that long to have kids and raise them, make things with your two hands, and create a story that will be shared in history books for years to come.

Life is fleeting, and that's what makes it awesome. I'm not a religious person, and some people find it sad that I don't believe I'll fly to an eternal place when I die. If you believe in heaven, reincarnation, or an afterlife of any sort, that's great! I don't judge or dismiss your beliefs. For me, though, what keeps me going is actually the idea that there is nothing else after this. It encourages me to make every day as incredible as I can, because time keeps going whether I sit on my couch all day or go out and try to explore somewhere new.

My existential crises develop when I feel like I'm not living up to life's potential, not necessarily my potential, but taking advantage of what life has to offer. Whether or not you have a ton of innate skills you could practice and develop over time, you can still immerse yourself in the beauty of this planet. There are forests, beaches, and mountains to walk around in. You can eat things that grow up out of the ground! You can explore all the nooks and crannies of a city that's existed for centuries before your birth. You have so many options available to you, it's straight up irresponsibly stupid to ignore them. And you're smart, so don't do that!

"By recording your dreams and goals on paper, you set in motion the process of becoming the person you most want to be. Put your future in good hands — your own."
- Mark Victor Hansen

GOAL SETTING

Going after your dreams on a tight schedule can make things even harder. You might have a school schedule, full time job, and/or kids to take care of on top of trying to make your dreams come true. I get it. That's why it's important to be realistic! That doesn't mean you shouldn't be optimistic, but I want you to build up your confidence. Start on the smaller scale, and reward yourself for everything that you finish. Remember that everything is progress. Figure out what is doable, and stick with it. A couple hours a week over the course of a year is a hundred hours of time put into your biggest fantasy, instead of just putting it off till tomorrow, which unfortunately turns into "never" for too many people.

Don't be afraid to say "no" to people while you're working your butt off! Knowing your boundaries and priorities is important, and tactfully declining to take on an extra non-mandatory work load will save you so much time and stress. You'll thank yourself later for having the guts to say "NO!"

That being said, "Yes" is just as important. It's possible great opportunities will come at inopportune times, but they may also be once in a lifetime events! If working extra hard for two months will get you to where you need to be, it's probably worth it! Get out and allow opportunities to present themselves to you. They say opportunity can come knocking on your door, but I don't know how she'll know where you live if you don't get out there and meet her first!

Being organized is a huge part of reaching your goals. You need to write down your goals and the steps for how to get there. Make sure that you're managing your time, both personal and professional. Have all your resources and materials in order and readily available! You never know what might happen.

Pick one of the goals you wrote above, star it, and break it down into five more "baby" steps you would need to achieve first.

1.
....

2.
....

3.
....

4.
....

5.
....

If any of those need to be broken down further, go ahead and make a note of it! Make a game plan for how you're going to get what you want! Set a deadline, create a reward system, and a measurable schedule that you can record your progress on.

I find deadlines to be very helpful because I'm a huge procrastinator. If I don't have a deadline, it's way less likely to get done. Even if you're not a procrastinator, deadlines can still help you stay organized and create schedules for incremental goals and to do lists. It's good to say, "I want to publish a book before my next birthday," but take it from me - you're going to sincerely benefit from breaking that giant goal down into many smaller ones.

Reward systems are helpful, too, but need to be very personal to you. You might have to do some guess and test work to figure out the most motivational system for you. For example, if you get everything done in one week you can go out and get crazy with friends or take yourself to get a pedicure. Moreover, if you work for forty-five minutes straight then you get a fifteen minute break to watch TV, text, or play a video game. For a visual representation, you could make a chart to give yourself stickers for completing projects. It could be as simple as getting to eat a piece of chocolate every time you cross something off your list.

I can't tell you what will work best for you, but it needs to be something that you enjoy enough to be an incentive but not something that you enjoy so much it would distract you from future work. Timelines are important, too. You might be better at focusing on one project for an hour or an entire day's worth of work. Try different techniques and figure out what works.

"Where attention goes energy flows; where intention goes energy flows!" – James Redfield

MANIFESTING

Having a positive attitude won't cure a disease and wishing you were famous won't make it happen overnight. Just because your dreams won't come true from wishing them as you blow out your birthday candles doesn't mean manifestation isn't effective or worth your time.

I believe meeting the universe (more than) halfway is necessary. You have to put in a ton of work to make your dreams come to fruition, but just starting to say what you want is a very important step. Say what you want from this life, and say it often. Use different external stimuli to remind yourself of your dreams. For example, whenever I see 11:11 on a clock I make a wish. Catching 11:11 is a reminder to say my hopes and dreams to myself. It keeps me in check. You can do the same thing when you run a yellow light, see a shooting star, or turn your light out before you go to bed.

Identifying what you want is an important first step. If you don't know what your end game is, there's not much point in manifesting your desires. It also helps to write down why you want to achieve these goals. What good are these goals serving you? There are probably a few overarching missions in your life that dictate most of your goals. Do you want to be healthy or help others? Make sure your goals are fulfilling those general driving forces for your life's purpose.

Creating an inspiration and/or mood board is a great activity to try once you know what goals you have. Cutting up magazines, and pinning physical words and images to a bulletin board above your desk or in a notebook can be a great reminder of where you want to get to and why. Take an afternoon to make something gorgeous.

After you're sure what it is you want, believe that it's possible! Expect your dreams can come true. If you don't believe it you'll create a self fulfilling prophecy. You can make a detailed five year plan with an organized scheduled to do list, but if you don't think you're capable of achieving your goals nothing good will happen.

Use your imagination to figure out how it would feel if your dream came true! What if you had your own business, a new home, or that ideal significant other? What would your day be like? What emotions would you experience? How would things be better and different?

The law of attraction is a real thing. We think tens of thousands of thoughts every day. Use those thoughts for promoting joy and a fun, healthy, successful future instead of self deprecating sabotage that makes you stagnant. Rewire how you think! Use your skills of thinking positively about yourself to thinking positively about your future.

When practicing the law of attraction, you also want to be calm and grateful. Meditate on a regular basis and thank the universe for what you already have. Say thank you out loud, and trust that the universe will meet you halfway.

To be successful, the first thing to do is fall in love with your work. – Sister Mary Lauretta

ENJOY HOW YOU MAKE MONEY

Most people have to work. There's only a very small percentage of people who are well off enough financially to not keep a job. Betting you need a steady income isn't a radical gamble, but variables like how much money you need to make, and how you'll make an income come from too many channels to count. You might live at home and just need to worry about having enough money to cover day to day expenses. You might have to pay for everything in your life yourself, including your rent, utilities, food, medicine, clothes, etc. You might have a partner you can split your expenses with, or you might have to cover the cost of not just your life, but others, like your children or live-in family members.

Based on your needs, you might have one part time job or two full time ones! Everyone's situation is different, and your financial needs and place(s) of employment will vary over your lifetime. The only consistent assumption is that you will need to have a job, and that job is going to take up a significant portion of your life.

In America, the run of the mill job is forty hours a week, which doesn't factor in prep work to get dressed, commute, or do extra projects or events outside of "the office". Let's say everything together is about fifty hours. There are only one hundred and twenty hours in the work week, including sleep. Do you really want to spend more than half of your waking hours in a state of unhappiness and stress? A job is a commitment if only because you're dedicating so much of your time to it, so being miserable or even tolerating your conditions really isn't any way to live.

If you hate your day job, you should be doing something else. It's honestly that simple. Right now there might not be a feasible plan where you can up and quit your day job. I may be a dreamer, but there needs to be a priority of paying rent and making sure you and your family can eat. You can still slowly use your free time to create a plan of action for going after something different. Your plan might be for changing professions, starting your own business, or just changing employers within the same industry. The point is, being miserable in your day job is unacceptable.

When I started my job at the psychiatric rehab center, I had no idea what I was getting into. I was hired after an internship because they liked me, too many people were fired or quit at the same time, and they were in a bind. Two dollars above minimum wage sounded like a dream to my nineteen-year-old-self, and I agreed in a heartbeat.

I worked there for five years and wore many different hats. I was a part of the restructuring of my program. It allowed the staff to wear fewer hats, focus on their work, and do a better job. I loved what I did for the most part. I enjoyed working with the population of mentally ill adults and creating curriculums for teaching classes on daily living skills and art. It was a good balance of interpersonal interaction, teaching, and paperwork but I knew that it wasn't something I wanted to do forever.

When people asked me what I wanted to do after I graduated from college, I told them I was going to get a raise, work as many hours as I could, and save up a ton of money so I could write a book and quit my job. I wanted to open up a glitter bar, sit on a rock painted like a rainbow and tell people they were beautiful. I wanted to make money from my blog and be a motivational speaker. I didn't have a business plan in place, but I knew I wasn't going to work there forever.

I was about a year into my plan post-graduation and saving as much money as I could. I wasn't unhappy with my job by any means, but all of a sudden, I went through a break up. My world was spun on its head after being with someone for almost seven years. I didn't know how to handle my day to day experiences anymore. I was heartbroken and empty, running everywhere on auto pilot. I despised leaving work because I had to go home instead of to his house. It felt strange and upset me every single day.

I made a decision to change my entire life. I wanted to shake up the structure of my life so I wouldn't realize what was missing. If everything was different, I wouldn't notice what was lacking. I put in a month's notice at my job and received a ton of support from my bosses and coworkers, for which I am eternally grateful.

In hindsight, this was not a good business decision. I didn't have as much money saved as I wanted to and I didn't have a concrete business plan in place. I was heartbroken, so the first few months of self-employment was spent doing more partying than working on my business. If I had stayed at my day job longer, I think I could have started my business in a stronger way.

In hindsight, this was the best personal decision I could have made. I don't regret it at all. I might not have planned as much as I could, but I gave myself exactly what I needed. In addition to healing from my break up, I also decreased my stress level significantly. I had no idea that such a high level of stress had become my baseline. As much as I had loved my day job, it wasn't exactly easy. I was constantly needed in a hundred different directions. There's a reason the burnout rate in the psychiatric industry is so high.

I didn't realize I had been so consistently stressed until I wasn't going to work every day. It makes me question the stress everyone is holding in on a daily basis at their jobs and in their lives. It makes me wonder what kind of physical ailments would have come my way if I had kept up the way I was going.

There are times we need to make decisions to take shitty jobs to make money to survive. Everyone's situation is different, and I don't mean to imply that you can just get angry at your job, flip a table, walk out and everything will be fine. If everyone did that, society would stop functioning. We need people to make food, clean buildings, deliver medical care, book appointments, and show up when someone calls 911. My point is, if you are in a state of misery and stress at your job, there are always other options to seek out. A change of pace in your work life can be as beneficial as a weekend at the spa, even if it's still not your dream job. As my obnoxiously optimistic and fictional friend Chris Traeger from *Parks And Recreation* would point out, "You have several options. They're all terrible, but you have them." Honestly though, don't let yourself get stuck. Don't quit your daydream.

"The secret of getting ahead is getting started." – Mark Twain

FINDING MOTIVATION

Going after what you really want is kind of terrifying. When I first quit my job, I made an appointment with a career counselor who was supposed to help me create a business plan and put it into action. I went in there and told the man all the things I wanted to do with my business and he sighed and stared at me. He told me that doing that many things was impossible, and there was no way I would be successful.

I nodded a lot because the lump in my throat let me know that if I went to speak I'd start crying. I clumsily gathered my papers and walked quickly to my car. I bawled the entire way home and tumbled into my house like a Peanuts character. I was sad the entire day, and then I got angry. I threw my papers across the room and thought, "Fuck him. I'm going to do this and he'll see it's possible."

So I am. I'm trying, anyway. I'm still nowhere near where I'd ideally like to be, but every month, every year gets better. I've learned so much about business, blogging, and community since I decided to hire myself, and I regret nothing. That doesn't mean I lost motivation sometimes, though.

Every day is different. Sometimes I wake up early with enough gusto to stroll right into the White House like I own the place, and other days I wake up and literally go back to sleep. What sucks about working for yourself is you can't call out. Well, you can, but nothing gets done. There's no one who can "pick up your shift". Every day is a decision to be productive, and that's a lot of pressure.

Finding motivation is an issue whether you're working for yourself, trying to start a new project, or trying to get up the gumption to complete the tasks your boss is giving you. My first suggestion is to get inspired. If you're lacking motivation, you're probably also lacking excitement. Take a break and do something that's been known to inspire you before. Maybe it's going for a run, wandering around a new part of a city, or laying in a field to watch the clouds roll past you. People find inspiration in all different places, so go to a place that's worked for you before and try to fill your soul with wonder.

Deadlines don't work for everyone, but I personally find them to be very helpful. I feel more and more people are becoming really skilled at procrastinating (maybe because of all the technology we have at our fingertips?), so plenty of people don't even start their projects till right before they're due. That insinuates if you didn't have a deadline, it wouldn't get done at all! So give yourself a deadline. There may not be a "consequence" for not completing it on time, especially if it's just for yourself, but it's likely just that act of missing the deadline will make you schedule it with more sincerity next time.

Another way to motivate yourself is to hang out with productive people. The other night, my friend was over and she was painting on my bed for a few hours as I worked on projects at my desk. She asked me if I wanted her to move or leave and I said, "No, actually your being there is forcing me to work so this is positive for everyone." It doesn't need to be that direct, though. Many times I will go home after spending time with a creative individual and feel inspired to start working on my own stuff.

It's a good example of using envy to create action in your life. If I see someone who has used their mind and hands to make something fantastic, I get a little jealous. There are two reactions to have in this situation: I could start spiraling, letting my inner monologue take over which tells me I'm pathetic, lazy, and have nothing to offer my friends or society. Or I could go home and get out art supplies to make something of my own, something I'm proud of that gives me hope for the future.

If none of that is working, just try doing something. Anything. Depending on your comfort level with unfinished projects, it can sometimes be helpful to have many projects going at once. That way, if you don't feel like working on Project B you can shift focus to Project D. I know plenty of people who can't deal with lingering projects, though, because it feels incomplete in their minds and like they're unnecessarily procrastinating.

It doesn't need to be related to your work or a To Do list. It can be cleaning your room, reorganizing the magnets on your refrigerator, or taking a walk. Taking a walk sounds trite because it's on every list of things to do, but maybe there's a reason for it. Many great minds have gained clarity through walking, like Einstein. If I lay in bed getting mad at Netflix for asking me if I'm "still there", I'm not going to magically feel motivated. If I force myself to put on shoes and leave the house, even braless in my pajamas, it helps.

"Nobody can give you wiser advice than yourself."
– Marcus Tullius Cicero

RECEIVING ADVICE

Trying is the key. Try a bunch of things and know it's okay if none of them work. One time I was at work, falling asleep at my desk because I hadn't slept in forty hours. They were sending me home, but wanted to make sure I'd make it home safe so my coworkers Googled "how to stay awake while driving". The site listed a bunch of suggestions, including "roll the windows down", but after that specific piece of advice there was a disclaimer that said, "*Be careful: this one may not work!" I laughed for ten minutes at the absurdity of it, which was actually what ended up keeping me awake enough to drive home. But the thing is, any suggestion might not work.

Advice you get from your best friend, car salesman, or great grandfather can completely suck. My advice is you should try (reasonable) suggestions once. If it feels terrible, chuck it out the window and never revisit it again. I've received advice which seemed absolutely bizarre, but after I tried it, found out it worked for me. That said, advice comes from personal experience. If you're not interested in the lifestyle of the advice giver, you also might not be interested in their advice. Your life is yours, and I think you should follow your gut more than anything else. That might seem counterintuitive coming from a book you'd find in the Self Help section, following paragraphs that give you suggestions on how to find motivation. But maybe it's not.

Maybe the best way to love yourself is to take what you want and leave the rest, to draw inspiration from select sources to make your own version of magic. There's way too much stimulus to take it all in and apply it to yourself. Work deliberately, and remember you're already doing an amazing job.

"Dwelling on the negative simply contributes to its power."
– Shirley MacLaine

DEALING WITH NEGATIVITY

If you go after your dreams, you're going to have critics. You're going to have people shit talking you behind your back and to your face. Depending on the nature of your dreams, you might have to deal with nasty e-mails, passive aggressiveness in meetings, or entire online threads about how much people hate you.

We all struggle with the concept, at least in the beginning, that we're under-qualified and have no idea what we're doing. You might not have the experience someone ten years your senior has, but you are qualified. You are important and you have the enthusiasm to be in this position in the first place, so you need to trust yourself. Trust you're here for a reason and you will enhance your skills as life goes on. Have faith that you will know where to find help if you need it, and know that asking for help doesn't make you a fake or inadequate.

How many times have you heard someone say, "I could have made that," as a passing judgment of an art piece? Maybe they could have! That's fine. The thing is, they didn't. Enthusiasm will beat out raw talent every time. If you're really skilled at something but don't utilize it, you won't succeed. If you try your heart out, you will. It's that simple.

It's hard to ignore really negative comments. We're all human, full of emotion and sensitivity, and it's almost impossible to let mean things roll off our backs. What's important is you bounce back. A couple of weeks ago, I received the nastiest e-mail I've ever gotten. I curled up in my boyfriend's bed and spent hours rotating between crying, delivering a negative monologue to myself, and feeling like a zombie. I worked through my feelings about the message a stranger felt they needed to send me and I made decisions about how I want to do my job and appear to the world.

I won't tell you to never listen to critics. Sometimes they can point out things you didn't realize you were(n't) doing, and they can also help you build a thicker skin to future negativity. If something really hits a chord with you, do some soul searching to figure out why. Is it bothering you because you realized you've strayed away from your vision, or is it upsetting you because you don't want to hear anything negative about yourself?

You're going to encounter negativity. It might be a direct attack against you, or it might be from a friend or family member you see all the time in social situations. It might be on the internet or in person. It might be off-handed or delivered by a third party. Know it's okay to get upset and dwell on it for a bit if you want. It's also important to figure out why it's bothering you in the first place, and decide what you're going to let affect you.

Fabulous people don't worry about what's being said behind their backs. They don't waste time finding out what's been said and getting anxious about how they're perceived. They're out living life the way they want. Love who you are and be that person so fully and unapologetically that you literally don't have time to worry about negative nonsense.

"Celebrating your achievements and applauding your triumphs is a sure way to refuel your enthusiasm and keep yourself motivated for your future endeavors." - Rooplen

CELEBRATING YOUR SUCCESS

You're awesome and you're going to do awesome things. Being excited about your inherent awesomeness isn't a bad thing, and you should be able to do it without feeling guilty. People might think you're narcissistic for congratulating yourself or sharing your successes, but you can't let that keep you from celebrating yourself and your life!

In terms of social media, I'd say to keep it in moderation. Posting every single day about how lucky you are to be in a "perfect" relationship can make people feel alienated and angry. That said, people love to celebrate with others! When I ran my Kickstarter for this book, I felt really guilty about posting so frequently about it. I thought I would be annoying everyone when I wrote about meeting my goals. I was overwhelmed by the support I got from people I had never even met who were happy to see me succeed.

If someone doesn't want to celebrate your success with you, or at least watch you do it on your own, they don't have to interact with you. They don't have to follow you on Twitter and they don't have to come to dinner with you. Non-supportive people will gradually filter out of your life in a natural way. If someone can't be happy for you because of their own hang-ups or jealousy, they don't deserve you in their life.

You should take that as a lesson to praise your friends for their success in life, too! Celebrate people the way you would want to be celebrated and that, like kindness, will come back around to you in turn.

Celebrating success doesn't just need to be about giant bucket list goals, either. Create your own reward system for getting excited about little accomplishments. It's not childish to praise yourself for folding your laundry or waking up without hitting the snooze button. Taking the high road in an argument or cooking a delicious dinner are achievements of their own. You are allowed to dance in your chair, sing loudly, and text your friends to tell them what good thing you just did.

MOVING FORWARD

I want you to believe in yourself. I want you to go after what you really want, even if you fail. I want you to try and constantly progress in your journey of self love and personal development. You are never going to peak, you will only constantly improve. Your setbacks do not define you or take away from what you've already accomplished. You are incredibly brilliant and sexy. You have the power in you to create the life you dream of. People who meet you are lucky. You will inspire everyone you meet. You should be proud of your life and love who you are. If you don't right now, you can and you will. If you don't right now, know that I do. I love you; amazing, weird, beautiful you.

THINGS TO TRY:

- Make an inspiration/mood board
- Organize your desk, studio, bedroom, closet
- Make a playlist to listen to while you're working
- Create a reward system for when you check things off your to do list
- Make a bucket list
- Make a fuck-it list (a list of things you never want to try)
- Say affirmations about your future
- Ask the universe for what you want out loud
- Carry around a citrine stone to manifest prosperity
- Post your accomplishments online
- Wake up early every day for a week and see how much you get done
- Evaluate why criticism/negativity upsets you
- Create deadlines and schedules for your goals
- Write your big goal down and tape it up somewhere where you'll see it often
- Take "before" photos
- Share your goal with friends who will hold you accountable
- Dedicate time every day to your goal
- Join a support group or community who can assist you with achieving your dreams
- Read articles, blogs, magazines, etc. about your industry or books by successful people
- Stop complaining
- Try standing up to work instead of sitting
- Shut down social media while you work so you're not distracted
- Write down the ideal scenario of you achieving your dreams and what great things would happen as a result
- Focus on the benefits of reaching your goal instead of the hardships or what you're sacrificing in the meantime
- Practice self love, compassion, and acceptance always

10 COMMANDMENTS OF SELF LOVE

1. Be positive and believe good things will happen.

2. Take care of yourself first and understand your non-negotiable needs.

3. Celebrate (little) things as much as you can.

4. Make your mental health a priority.

5. Practice creativity every day.

6. Create a fabulous support system.

7. Embrace everything that makes you unique.

8. Be as kind to yourself as you would be to your best friend.

9. Dream big and never stop making goals.

10. Accept who you are right now, even if there's room for improvement.

SONGS ABOUT SELF LOVE

- "Freckles" by Natasha Bedingfield
- "Video" by India Arie
- "You Learn" by Alanis Morissette
- "Transgender Dysphoria Blues" by Against Me!
- "Unstoppable" by Kerrie Roberts
- "I Feel Beautiful" by Fantastia
- "Who Says" by Selena Gomez featuring The Scene
- "Dancing On My Own" by Robyn
- "Who You Are" by Jessie J
- "Sexy And I Know It" by LMFAO
- "Titanium" by David Guetta featuring Sia
- "Stronger" by Kelly Clarkson
- "I Love Myself Today" - Bif Naked
- "Unpretty" by TLC
- "Brave" by Sara Bareilles
- "Express Yourself" by Madonna
- "Everybody Is A Star" by Sly And The Family Stone
- "The Climb" by Miley Cyrus
- "Roar" by Katy Perry
- "Bulletproof" by La Roux
- "Born This Way" by Lady Gaga
- "I'm Real" by J. Lo + Ja Rule
- "Greatest Love Of All" by Whitney Houston
- "Shine" by Anna Nalick
- "Hero" by Mariah Carey
- "That's Why You're Beautiful" by Beyonce
- "Hold Your Head Up" by Argent

- "I Am Not My Hair" by India Arie
- "Pocketfull Of Sunshine" by Natasha Bedingfield
- "Superwoman" by Alicia Keys
- "We R Who We R" by Ke$ha
- "Beautiful" by Christina Aguilera
- "I Will Survive" by Gloria Gaynor
- "I Am Not A Robot" by Marina And The Diamonds
- "Miss Independent" by Ne-Yo
- "Extraordinary Machine" by Fiona Apple
- "Gold" by Britt Nicole
- "I Love Myself" by Kendrick Lamar
- "Fuckin' Perfect" by Pink
- "Firework" by Katy Perry
- "What Makes You Beautiful" by One Direction
- "I Believe I Can Fly" by R. Kelly
- "Shake It Off" by Taylor Swift
- "Can't Hold Us Down" by Christina Aguilera
- "Love Me For Me" by Ashlee Simpson
- "All I Do Is Win" by DJ Kahled
- "Not So Average" by V. Rose
- "Flawless" by Beyonce
- "Unwritten" by Natasha Bedingfield
- "Float On" by Modest Mouse
- "Not A Pretty Girl" by Ani DiFranco
- "Secrets" by Mary Lambert
- "Fight Song" by Rachel Platten

RESOURCES

Chapter 2 - Gratitude & Positivity
SARK, planetsark.com
Gretchen Rubin, gretchenrubin.com
100 Happy Days, 100happydays.com
Soul Pancake, soulpancake.com

Chapter 3 - Self Care
Directory of HAES Practitioners, haescommunity.org
Babe Vibes, babevibes.com

Chapter 5 - Staying Creative
Magical Daydream, magicaldaydream.com
Color Me Katie, colormekatie.blogspot.com
The House That Lars Built, thehousethatlarsbuilt.com
Keri Smith, kerismith.com
Plus Size Clothing: ASOS, Forever 21, We Love Colors

Chapter 6 - Connecting
Myers Briggs Personality Test, 16personalities.com
Enneagram Personality Test, enneagraminstitute.com
Love Language Test, 5lovelanguages.com

Chapter 7 - Embracing Your Weird
Improv Everywhere, 16personalities.com
Veronica Varlow, dangerdame.com
Burning Man, burningman.org

Chapter 8 - Self Acceptance
Anastasia Amour, anastasiaamour.com
Gala Darling, galadarling.com
The Militant Baker, themilitantbaker.com

Chapter 9 - Dreams & Goals
Day Zero Project, dayzeroproject.com
Femtrepreneur, femtrepreneur.co

ACKNOWLEDGMENTS

Thanks to my dad for giving every ounce of support he could have possibly given me and never allowing me to believe that an obstacle was the end of the road.

Thanks to Ashley Knight for being my partner in crime and always reminding me of fun if I ever forget. I adore your mind and soul, but mostly your hot body.

Thanks to Joe Kuhlman for loving me without judgments and holding me when I go crazy. You have taught me so much about love, relationships, and companionship and I'm forever grateful to you for your ongoing support and surprises.

Thanks to Cristen Hoyt for helping me accept my own weird and showing me I can actually be of service in the area of self help. After this we should probably go get a snack.

Thanks to Charlotte Boyer for demonstrating that friendship holds out through every transformation, adjustment, and drunken night. Pencil me in for every spring solstice until you die.

Thanks to Maura Housley for being so thoughtful, professional, talented, and enthusiastic about creating beautiful images and making my dream tangible.

Thanks to Heather Hackett for being such a badass editor and giving me a boost of confidence when I needed it the most.

Thanks to Bryan Yingling for agreeing to make my words look pretty inside this book instead of me just stapling together a bunch of cut up Word documents. You are the definition of party, sir.

Thanks to Janice Jedrowicz for pimping out my Kickstarter and helping me come up with the name of the book. If I ever get on a talk show it will be because of your unfaltering faith in me.

Thanks to April Gomez for being a role model for who I want to be when I never grow up. The way you make decisions, live life, and have fun is a walking lesson for all of us.

Thanks to Katie Sokoler for showing me what life could be like if I decided to let my imagination affect my reality, and getting me through so many tough nights without even realizing it. The raindrop photo is for you.

Thanks to LaShandra Oliver for accepting my resignation with grace and support, making me feel excited about my scary decision to try to be my own person sans day job.

Thanks to Joe Kuhlman, Ashley Knight, Cristen Hoyt, and Judy Cox for being models for Maura's photos.

Thanks to Maria Waksmunski for finding my Kickstarter and offering me a gig with her publishing team at Mascot.

Thanks to every single backer of my Kickstarter campaign that made publishing this book possible.

And finally, thanks to Bug. You're cute as hell.